Trick Training for Horses

Bea Borelle with Gudrun Braun

Trick Training for Horses

Fun Ways to Engage, Challenge, and Bond with Your Horse

Translation by Kristina McCormack

TRAFALGAR SQUARE
North Pomfret, Vermont

First published in 2011 by
Trafalgar Square Books
North Pomfret, Vermont 05053

Printed in China

Originally published in the German language as *Bea Borelles Zirkusschule* by Franckh-Kosmos Verlags-GmbH & Co. KG, Stuttgart

Library of Congress Cataloging-in-Publication Data

Borelle, Bea.
  [Bea Borelles Zirkusschule. English]
  Trick training for horses : fun ways to engage, challenge, and bond with your horse / Bea Borelle with Gudrun Braun.
      p. cm.
  Includes index.
  ISBN 978-1-57076-462-2
  1. Horses--Training. 2. Circus animals--Training. I. Braun, Gudrun. II. Title.
  SF287.B67 2011
  636.1'0835--dc22
                        2010040719

All photos by Alain Laurioux/Kosmos *except*: p. xi *top* (courtesy of Bea Borelle); pp. ix *bottom*, 47 (Christiane Slawik); pp. xiv, 10, 18, 19, 20, 21, 22, 23, 40, 55 *middle and bottom*, 46, 48, 49, 52, 58, 59, 65 *middle*, 76, 111 (Cristiane Slawik/Kosmos); pp. iii, ix, 96, 117, 132 (J&G Toton)

Cover design by RM Didier
Typefaces: Strada, Scala, Scala Sans, Scala Sans Condensed

10 9 8 7 6 5 4 3 2 1

> Contents

Foreword by Philippe Karl   vii

Introduction   viii

My Horses   xi

Recommended Reading   xiii

The Basics   xiv

What Is Trick Training?   1
What Kind of Horse Can
    Be Taught Tricks?   1

"Hands-On" Praise   25
Food Rewards   26
Pausing   28
Ignoring   29
Punishment   29
Duration and Intensity of Training 30
Commands   30
Saying "No"   33
Differentiating between Exercises   33
The "On" and "Off" Switches   33
Which Tricks to Teach?   36
Starting Point to End Goal   37
Making Connections   38
Going Back a Step or Two   39

Where to Train   5
Equipment   6
Why Train Your Horse Tricks?   10
The Learning Environment
    and Communication   14
Ramifications for Riding   18

The Trick Training System   24

Atmosphere   25
Verbal Praise   25

Reviving the Riding Horse with
    Trick Training Methodology   40

The Basic Course for Riders   41

Trick Training—
    The Foundation   46

Basic Exercises   47
The Statue   47
Backing-Up   50
Stepping Sideways   53

Tricks for Bombproof Horses   55

Riding without a Bridle   56
Statue with "Racket Sack"   58
In Motion with "Racket Sack"   60
Statue with Umbrella   62
Statue with Buckets   64
Statue with Sheet   67

Tricks for Brave Horses   69

The "Ribbon Wall"   71
Standing on Pallets or a Pedestal   73
The Balance Beam   76
The Tightrope   78

Tricks for Horses with a Sense of Humor   80

Crossing the Forelegs   81
Unrolling and Rolling-Up Carpet   82
Nudging and Pushing   87
Carrying Objects   89
Under the Covers   92
"Unsaddled"   94

Classic Tricks   96

Classic Trick Basics   97
Plié   97
One-Legged Bow
   (without "Leg Rope")   103
One-Legged Bow (with "Leg Rope")   107
Kneeling   113
Lying Down "Upright" (or "Awake")   115
Lying Down "Flat" (or "Asleep")   126
Sitting   128

Something More I Want to Say   132

Index   133

> Foreword by Philippe Karl

October 8, 1998, marks the first time I saw Bea and her pony Ben working together—it was at a three-day clinic Bea had organized. I observed the two attentively, without saying a word. I was impressed, because the pair radiated an accomplished solidarity and kinship that is rare and seldom seen in the horse world.

When I think of Bea and her horses, I think of the story of *The Little Prince* by Antoine de Saint-Exupéry. In the story, the little prince asks the narrator to draw him a sheep. The narrator, after several failed attempts, instead draws a simple box, and offers it to the prince explaining the sheep that he asked for is inside. The prince enthusiastically accepts this, even peering closer at the drawing, wondering aloud if the sheep will eat much grass and noting that it "has gone to sleep."

In real life, Bea is a "little princess." She remains alive with creativity and imagination, such as that found in the little prince of Saint-Exupéry's story. She maintains a childlike freshness and willingness to "play" that most adults lack because they are intent on taking themselves seriously. It is this innate "understanding"—so evident in Bea—that the narrator discovers in the little prince (but not in the adults he meets), and that I believe is sadly missing from the world of riding and training horses.

I encourage all riders and trainers to try Bea's methods. You will rediscover some of the "magic" of your childhood and see how it can change the way you work with horses. Trick training may not seem "serious enough" for "serious riders," but it is the means of helping humans make more of their horses than athletes or beasts of burden—it is one of the best ways to make your horse your friend.

French riding master Philippe Karl is the founder of the École de Légèreté ("school of lightness"), a three-year training course based on the principle of "absolute respect of the horse." His philosophy is intended to apply to all breeds of horses and all riding disciplines. He is the author of several books and DVDs.

> Introduction

Dear Horse Lovers,

First of all, I would like to thank you.

You are the impetus for a renewed reflection on my work with horses. This has helped me achieve more clarity and precision in my work. I now approach horse training with greater awareness—with your potential questions as a reader and student always in the back of my mind.

Before you bought this book, you surely looked at other works on the topic of trick training. How does what I do with my horses differ from what my colleagues do? I think my insights, experiences, and conclusions about trick training are worth reading and emulating because my goal is for you and your horse to feel encouraged, enabled, and enthusiastic about your work—whatever it may be. You and your horse will discover what fun these exercises are, and through them you will develop a greater partnership, noticeable even early in the trick-training process.

Through trick training, you can learn how to make your horse enthusiastic about his "serious" work. You will experience for yourself why tricks are worthwhile for the general education of your horse, regardless of your chosen discipline. In fact it is my own heartfelt desire to convey how the most difficult of disciplines—dressage, for example—can be "joyfully advanced" with the help of these exercises. Trick training lets us experience precisely how quickly horses learn and understand. These realizations are relevant to the training of the much more complex and complicated lessons under saddle. In addition, trick training helps to motivate horses to be "achievers" and enables them to willingly perform schooling exercises that are otherwise likely to bore them.

In this book, you will learn to pay careful attention to your horse's actions as he performs a trick.

You may have heard of me, or you may even have my DVDs *Circus School* (Volumes 1 and 2) on your shelf and have successfully tried one or more of the exercises in them. However, you may not know that I do not specialize exclusively in trick training—although it is, quite simply, a terrific experience to train horses in this way. My personal goal is to make horses "laugh." If, in addition, I can amuse my students and observers, then it is even more fun for me. Those who know me personally know that I am only grown up on the outside! Inside I am still a little girl who hates being bored and is always searching for some new diversion.

If you do not already know of my work, I would like to give you a brief introduction.

My repertoire stretches from the most basic education of a young horse to longeing, work in-hand, and work in long reins. It also includes the education of the rider, from a beginner's foundation through the equitation lessons of advanced dressage.

I began my study of trick training in the 1980s. Horse performances in circuses and other professional shows had always previously fascinated me, but my first real urge to try it for myself came while watching a performance at Equitana, the giant horse exposition in Essen, Germany. I can still vividly remember one odd and hilarious number, in which a horse laid down in a "bed" and pulled the covers over himself!

My reaction then was probably much like yours now: I asked myself whether I could in fact teach my own horse this exercise.

My first horse was an Anglo-Arabian mare named Monodie. Initially an extremely complicated and dangerous mare, she taught me how to train a horse solid, basic obedience from the ground. Later I also worked with her at liberty in a small arena—what today you would call a round pen. Monodie eventually became so obedient that she would change gait and direction, or stand as still as a statue for as long as I pleased, just from my voice commands. In principle, this is the same kind of training that you see in equestrian "spectaculars," liberty performances, and circuses.

Here I prepare to greet the audience, along with two of my fellow performers.

I took Monodie to the well-known dressage trainer Richard Hinrichs, and in addition to training in general dressage work, we learned exercises like the Spanish walk and the bow. Monodie was also taught to lie down flat and to sit on her haunches. After only a year, I could put together a short performance that included all these maneuvers.

At this time, I was also giving children riding lessons, and once a year I would put together a little "recital" for them to demonstrate what they learned to their parents. My performance with Monodie became an extra attraction during the recital, into which I also integrated exercises that I had learned from Linda Tellington-Jones' Tellington Method—for example, Monodie would walk through a fluttering curtain of streamers and over a low see-saw, and for a finale, I rode her bareback and bridleless (see my recommendations for books by Linda Tellington-Jones on p. xiii). This presentation was great fun for Monodie, the audience, and me.

Of all my current horses, my "famous" pony Ben has been with me and "connected" to me the longest.

In those days I also owned a pony mare named Schnucki, and I introduced her, too, to the world of tricks. It was 1991 when my now "famous" pony, Ben, came into my life, and once Ben acquired a solid foundation of basic training, I began teaching him tricks, too. Since then, this little gelding's repertoire has become so comprehensive that I have to keep a written list so I do not forget all the things he can do!

More recently, Ben's new friend Anouk has also begun learning tricks. Anouk was already so well educated that it was only our second day of getting to know one another when I successfully taught her to take a bow. In fact, through trick training she learned very quickly that she would receive praise and food for certain movements, and this made her curious about me—so she tried harder to form a relationship with me.

A similar situation occurs over and over again at my clinics. There I do not have the opportunity to intensively get to know the horses or to establish a trusting relationship in advance. I go directly to the horse and demonstrate how particular tricks are to be done. Through intensive praise and food rewards the result is always a successfully completed exercise. And anyone can achieve the same results once they know the tricks and how to teach them.

In the following chapters, I explain and demonstrate tricks that every horse can master. If you proceed in a careful, conscientious manner, these exercises are fun, safe, and will foster a new, intensive partnership between you and your horse.

When I first started training my horses tricks, there weren't any books or DVDs on the subject available. Now there are several, but I believe that my methods truly make trick training accessible to anyone, with any kind of horse. So, I must thank my co-author Gudrun Braun, whose tireless efforts helped make it possible to bring this book to life and bring my techniques to the public. Have fun reading, practicing, and performing tricks!

Bea Borelle

› My Horses

Monodie, Anglo-Arabian, foaled 1976

I got to know Monodie in 1980 when I leased her as a riding horse, and I bought her a year later. I rode her while working with well-known trainers including Kurt Schulge, Claus Penquitt, Richard Hinrichs, and throughout my training to become a TTEAM Practitioner with Linda Tellington-Jones. In 1996, I sold her to a student and Monodie lived out her twilight years with her.

Barros, Lusitano-cross gelding, foaled 1986

I met Barros in 1994 when I was working with Joaquim Barros in Portugal. In 1996 I bought him (then a stallion) and returned with him to Germany. In October of 2000 I had to have Barros euthanized because of an untreatable injury. This loss still haunts me to this day.

Ben, grade pony gelding, foaled 1989

Ben came to me in 1991. Since he was too small for me to ride, I trained him in-hand and focused on tricks. Since 2001 he has lived with me in Southern France (along with Tabea—see p. xii), and his training repertoire—in general (not only tricks)—has grown enormously. I believe Ben to be one of the most reliably versatile and well-trained ponies in the world.

Monodie—Anglo-Arabian mare.

(Left) Barros, a Lusitano-cross gelding and (right) Ben, a grade pony gelding.

Tabea, Trakehner mare, foaled 1997

I bought Tabea from the Webelsgrund Trakehner stud. She is out of Talinka von Karon and her sire is Monsieur AA. In 2001, I relocated to France with Tabea and Ben, and that year she had a serious accident requiring I take her out of training for three months. Since November of 2001, she has received an education that spans the spectrum—including under-saddle and in-hand work, and trick training.

Anouk, grade pony mare, foaled 1998

My sister gave me Anouk as a wedding gift in 2002. At the time, the mare was considered difficult and unrideable. Since she has been living with us in France, she has learned unbelievably quickly: she now free-longes, works in long reins and on the longe line, and already does a number of tricks like lying down, sitting, and taking a bow. She is beginning to piaffe and Spanish walk. In the meantime, she has also become a reliable ride at all gaits, and like Ben and Tabea, she jumps very well. The causes of her early difficulties seem to have been put to rest.

Ben—pony-cross gelding (top);
Anouk—grade pony mare (right);
and Tabea—Trakehner mare (left).

› Recommended Reading

I use Linda Tellington-Jones' Tellington Method in my own work with horses, and many of her techniques are very helpful when training your horse how to perform tricks. The following two books are available from Trafalgar Square Books (www.horseandriderbooks.com).

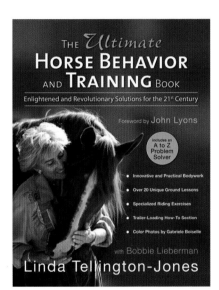

The Ultimate Horse Behavior and Training Book
Enlightened and Revolutionary Solutions for the 21st Century
Linda Tellington-Jones with Bobbie Leiberman

The definitive work of Linda Tellington-Jones, including everything you need to learn and practice the world-famous Tellington Method.

Getting in TTouch with Your Horse
How to Assess and Influence Personality, Potential, and Performance
Linda Tellington-Jones with Sybil Taylor

Linda shows you how to analyze your horse's physical traits in order to determine your horse's personality.

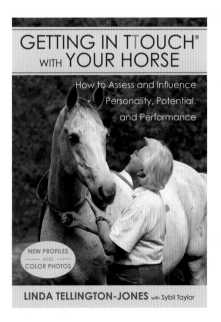

Trick Training— The Basics

› What Is Trick Training?

In school we learned that each new subject begins with a definition—that is, with a short description of the theme to be explored. Trick training is made up of maneuvers and "exercises" that originated in the circus. The concept of "circus" is derived from the "circle" or "ring" traditionally surrounded by onlookers who are presented with a program featuring animal training, acrobatics, and clowning. The program is meant to entertain or amaze people, or bring them to laughter or tears.

I actually prefer to call tricks "circus exercises" because the lessons I teach are indeed schooling exercises useful in establishing balance in the horse's training regimen—they are not solely for entertainment. However, in recognition of the more common and popular term, I will use "tricks" and "trick training" throughout this book.

Although many of these exercises may look spectacular, they are always based on the natural behaviors of the animals involved. Through appropriate training—along with praise and food rewards—the behaviors can be called up by a trainer at any time. Bowing and Kneeling, for example, are movements that can be observed in the horse in a natural setting. In the process of standing up after lying down, horses are sometimes happy to remain in the sitting position in order to leisurely give their belly a good scratch.

In many cases, tricks are static exercises: bowing, sitting down, and kneeling are postures that occur in one fixed place, and the horse remains in the position for a period of time. In addition, there are exercises in motion, such as Fetching and Retrieving an object, the Spanish Walk, Rolling, Waltzing, and Backing-Up. Furthermore, within the general category of tricks there are those that I call "classics," and then those that are the product of the trainer's imagination—like jumping through a ring of fire.

› What Kind of Horses Can Be Taught Tricks?

I can attest that *every* horse can be taught tricks. Of course, some have more fun with it than others. Some learn very quickly, while others only slowly find their way into the spirit of the lessons. This is totally natural.

Age The youngest horse that has attended one of my clinics was a six-month-old pony filly. In addition, I had a one-and-a-half-year-old Friesian stallion in one course that had already mastered several tricks. But, those are surely exceptions. Horses are not totally physically mature and ready for full work until they are seven years old.

However, at the age of three or four years, most breeds are well-enough developed that their education, including trick training, can begin. At this age, they possess sufficient mental maturity and the ability to concentrate so that learning comes easily.

It is important to note that older horses already very advanced in their training for a specific discipline can learn tricks, too. In many ways, these horses are the most grateful students because they are so happy to add variation to their training routine. Basically, you can teach an old horse new tricks! Of course, I do not mean all tricks are appropriate—selections should be determined by a horse's individual physical characteristics, state of health, and soundness. On the following pages I discuss which lessons are appropriate for which horses, as well as what kind of prerequisites must be established.

Ponies tend to be very easy to train to perform tricks.

Size　Over the years I have determined that the smaller the horse is, the more quickly he learns tricks. This is probably because smaller horses are easier to handle. In addition, ponies (for instance) tend to have a great deal of self-confidence and this means they may find the exercises less threatening than larger horses.

Another thing to keep in mind is that, from a purely physical point of few, a horse over 16 hands faces totally different challenges in Lying Down (getting his body down to the ground) than an 11-hand pony does. So, you might find it very difficult to teach the tall horse the Lying Down lesson. In cases where a horse's physical size impedes his ability to perform a trick, it may be best to avoid the particular exercise altogether.

Temperament and Intelligence　As far as temperament is concerned, horses that easily become overly excited or are prone to panic must be introduced to tricks in a relaxed and calm manner. Allow considerably more time for each lesson than with horses that are "quiet" and sure of themselves to begin with.

I find that, for the most part, the smaller "hot–blooded" horses are more intelligent in the area of trick training. This means that their education usually proceeds more quickly and their repertoire can be more comprehensive than that of their "cold-blooded" counterparts.

Breed and Gender　Breed and gender play a very small role when it comes to determining aptitude for tricks. However, whenever handling a dominant mare or a stallion, experience on the part of the trainer is an absolute necessity.

I often observe during my clinics that stallions and geldings that are relaxed drop their penises while working. Some owners are bothered by this, others are not (either way, it is obvious to the observers!) In no way do I interfere with this behavior. It does not bother me during everyday training, and I always plan to structure any formal presentation in such a way that geldings or stallions do not have the opportunity to "drop." I find that it is always during the "quieter" lessons that horses display this behavior.

Health and Soundness　Horses that are expected to perform stretching tricks—such as Plié, Bowing, Kneeling, or Spanish Walk—must be totally sound. I do not work horses that have stifle problems, for example, in any of the stretching or lengthening lessons, because I do not know how much that work could stress or harm them.

Rearing on command can add a dramatic flair to any performance.

Tricks promote self-confidence
in horses.

There is, however, a repertoire of tricks that work specifically for
the unsound or rehabilitating horse. For example, a lame horse that
can only be worked at the walk can learn such static exercises as
The Statue, Saying "Yes" or "No," Fetching and Retrieving, or Rolling Out the Carpet.

Prerequisites: Basic Training and Knowledge   Before begin-
ning a trick training program, it is very beneficial if your horse can
be safely led, and he should allow himself to be touched everywhere
on his body. The relationship between horse and trainer should be
free of anxiety, fear, or aggression. Many of my preparatory lessons
help pave the way for a good partnership and ensure an appropriate
atmosphere for calm, undisturbed learning (see p. 42).

You do have to be flexible, however. When Anouk came to me,
she was oversensitive. Her experience with humans had taught her
that they were pushy and demanding, and so she initially reacted
to me nervously, becoming panicked, or resorting to bucking and
rearing. Even though the mare did not know me well at first, I immediately built tricks into our daily schooling sessions because I
felt they would help her learn to trust me. It makes no difference
to me whether a horse first learns to back up, longe, work under
saddle, or perform tricks—whatever is best for him can be used as
a training tool.

If you follow my trick training program, you will find your horse will acquire a great willingness to learn—he will realize that learning can be fun!

Ben demonstrates a piaffe-pirouette.

> Where to Train

Training Space With appropriate footing, indoor arenas, outdoor arenas, and round pens are all very good places to practice. In a large indoor or outdoor arena I use ribbon or tape to create a smaller space to work in. I limit the space so that if my horse decides to wander off during the lesson, he cannot go very far. I advise against working in a totally unfenced area. Only an advanced trainer with a very well-schooled horse can be certain of obedience in such a scenario—for all others, too large a space brings only unnecessary frustration.

Using your horse's pasture or paddock for practice raises the question as to whether you can make it clear that the area for grazing, rest, and relaxation is now a work area. I don't find this to be a problem—horses can learn that when in my presence they may, should, and must work. When I depart, the pasture resumes its usual function. Practicing in the pasture also helps prepare me for the different challenges of public performances on grassy surfaces—for example, I prepared for a performance on a grass surface at the Leisure Riders Test Center in Reken, Germany, by working with my horses in their pasture.

You can also use a box stall or stable area as a training space if, for example, you have a horse that is bored because he is confined due to illness or injury. I have no qualms about doing whatever static tricks the horse's condition allows in such an enclosed space.

Footing Conditions In all lessons where the horse is to lower himself to the ground in any way, it is naturally very important that the footing conditions are comfortable. For example, many sensitive horses do not like to Bow, Kneel, or Lie Down on wood-chip footing.

Footing that is too soft and loose is not appropriate for sitting exercises—horses do not get the necessary support, their forelegs slide out from under them, and they can neither comprehend the lesson nor grasp what you are trying to make them understand.

For all other tricks the footing typically found in an indoor arena, or turf, is usually sufficient. While you work, notice whether your horse shows signs of discomfort, and if he does, move to a different workspace.

> Equipment

Equipment for the Horse

> The horse should wear a halter or longeing cavesson, or if you are going to combine tricks with riding in a performance, a bridle can be used.
> For leading I recommend the Tellington Method lead ropes, either with a chain or without, either of which you can thread through the halter (see p. xiii). Your lead rope should be 6 feet long and will be used for most lessons including the Statue, the One-Legged Bow, Plié, Lying Down, and Sitting.
> In addition, I use work on the longe line as preparation for training at liberty. Depending on whether a given exercise demands a greater or lesser degree of closeness to the horse, I will either use a lead rope or grasp a standard longe line at varying lengths. The longe line should always be attached to the horse's headstall—under no circumstances should it ever be directly linked to a bit.
>
> *Note:* I do not use lead or longe lines with panic snaps because when I hold the line very short, I could inadvertently trip the mechanism and open the snap.
> I use whips of varying lengths: from 4 feet long, to short crops, to your standard-length longe whips. For some exercises, a crop without a "floppy" end-piece is useful.
> For the Plié, One-Legged Bow, and Lying Down, a "leg rope" can be helpful. This is a broad, strong, soft rope or band, about 12 feet long, with an 3-inch "loop" at the end (see photo on p. 109).
> I also sometimes use leg wraps, and with very fidgety horses I use shipping boots on the forelegs.

Equipment for the Trainer

> The trainer should wear solid shoes. This is particularly important when practicing tricks that involve the horse lowering himself to the ground. I personally prefer shoes that protect my toes with a steel cap.
> I think it is important to wear long pants during training because there is always the chance of bodily contact with the horse, and skin abrasion or bruising can easily occur.
>
> On the other hand, during exhibitions my costume usually suits the theme. Sometimes I even wear a short skirt—but that's show time!

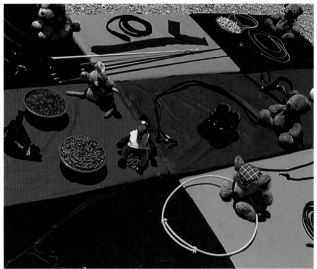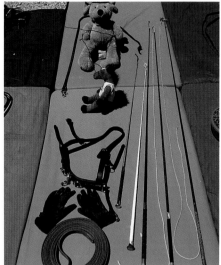

Lead ropes, longe lines, various whips and crops, gloves, and treats, all help you successfully train your horse tricks.

> Gloves, too, are recommended to protect your hands from rope burn when a lead or rein suddenly slides forcefully through them.
> If your horse gets fidgety during the bowing or kneeling exercises, you can protect your own shins by putting shipping boots on his forelegs. (If the reason the horse gets fidgety is fear, then review earlier work in-hand before attempting these tricks.)
> Use a small hip pouch (fanny pack) for storing treats.
> For performances, suitable costumes depend on the theme of your act and your unbounded imagination.

Food Rewards Your choice of treats plays a very large role in trick training. Perhaps your horse has a strong preference—one horse likes carrots, another prefers apples, and another chooses commercially made horse "cookies."

Even if you only practice a few exercises in the beginning (although you will want to add to your repertoire once you and your horse start having fun!), you should choose high quality treats. If you are currently working on one or two tricks, you only need a small quantity of food—but it should be very good and very flavorful.

I feed either carrot pieces (because of their high vitamin content) or commercially made treats. I use brands that I am certain

Here, the doll models "safety shoes" (steel-toed boots) like the ones I recommend. Protective footwear is a sensible precaution.

have high quality ingredients. When I work on a complex act or if I am training a horse tricks full-time, I use a great deal of food, and it becomes expensive. In such instances, I turn to pelleted feed from good quality producers. Other alternatives are cracked corn or hay cubes.

Moist or wet treats, such as carrots, apples, and other fruits, have the drawback of rotting or getting moldy when there are leftovers in your treat pouch at the end of a work session. I try to stay in the habit of emptying both my treat pouch and my pockets immediately after a lesson.

The actual quantity of food you use is very important to your training. I recommend giving frequent smaller portions instead of fewer larger ones. If commercially produced treats are too large for my purposes, I cut them up into pieces so that there are not long

A hip pouch (or fanny pack) is perfect for carrying an assortment of treats while you work.

pauses in the midst of a training session while my horse chews. I want to repeat the exercises in quick succession, rather than (and now I am exaggerating!) waiting several minutes while my horse finishes chewing before giving another cue. It is important to me that the horse stays focused throughout the learning process, rather than practically forgetting what he has learned because of prolonged snack breaks.

I give large portions—a whole carrot, for example—only when I want to give an extraordinary reward. I also use large, long carrots when I begin practicing the Plié or Bow—exercises in which the horse must bring his head deep between his forelegs and under his belly. He cannot see my hand when he is doing these tricks and could unintentionally nip my fingers reaching for a small treat.

› Why Train Your Horse Tricks?

Gymnastic Benefits My professional colleagues who also regularly use tricks in their horse training often name gymnastic effects as the greatest benefit of the practice. Personally, I think this aspect is overrated. I doubt that after 10 deep knee bends you would stand up and say, "That's my complete workout for today!"

Tricks that demand stretching and movement certainly further the health and fitness of the horse, but I let a horse perform a Bow, for example, a maximum of five times during one training session. If I work with him a second time on the same day, I will not go over that exercise again. If you take the concept of gymnastic training seriously, then you understand that it consists of sequences of movements that are much more complex and must be performed with greater regularity than any trick. For example, lateral movements—such as shoulder-in and haunches-in—are trained in a continual progression until the horse eventually masters them all in trot and canter. This is true gymnastic training.

Lateral movements, such as shoulder-in and haunches-in, "gymnasticize" the horse more than tricks ever will.

In classical dressage, for example, no movement exists for its own sake. Every exercise—whether the Spanish walk or rein-back—serves as a preparation for the next one and improves the trainer's previous work to the point of perfection. Tricks do not have this "progressive" quality. They exist for their own sake. Perfecting them will not necessarily improve other schooling exercises you do with your horse, whatever your discipline.

For example, the trick I call Atop the Mountain—where the horse brings his hind legs closer to his forelegs while standing on a pedestal—does not *gymnasticize* the horse, even though it *stretches* him. Although my horse Barros mastered this trick easily (even with a rider on his back), the stretching accomplished could not in any way improve his way of going (the quality of his gaits). The effects of a static exercise do not seem to carry over to the dynamics of movement. (Read more about Barros and this trick on p. 15.)

The one exception is the Spanish Walk, as practicing it regularly over a period of time can improve the piaffe and passage in upper level dressage horses, and so you could attribute a "gymnasticizing" effect to it. Despite this, in my view it is ridden work, including

Tabea performs Atop the Mountain (see p. 74).

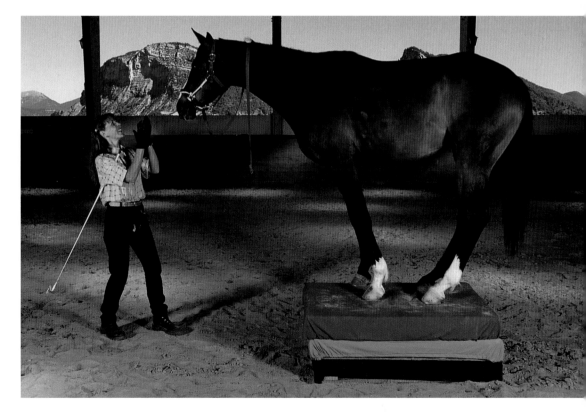

halting, rein-back, and lateral movements that develop a horse's ability to carry himself and collect—it is this kind of work that is similar to one of our own 45-minute workouts at a health club.

However, despite their lack of true gymnastic benefit, there are many very good reasons to do tricks.

What Do You Hope to Achieve? There are many good reasons to teach your horse tricks. Of course, there is the fact that teaching your horse unusual exercises is fascinating work, and the process can be humorous and enjoyable. But there are other reasons besides these:

To Deepen Your Relationship with Your Horse It makes sense that you not only broaden your horse's repertoire of tricks with these lessons but that you also get to know him much better than you would just sitting in the saddle. By doing this work, you learn to better assess and appreciate your horse's abilities. Observe your horse's expression as he practices the tricks he most enjoys. Horses' faces express a great deal about their overall well-being.

You'll be surprised by which tricks you and your horse enjoy most.

To Develop the Horse's Intelligence Tricks are another way of training the brain. Domestically kept horses are not nearly as challenged as those in the wild. Assuming you develop a progressively larger repertoire of tricks over time, horses become smarter and more clever through this kind of training. The more diverse the exercises, the more pronounced the effect. Once your horse has grasped the fact that he receives liberal praise and food for relatively little effort, his willingness to work increases enormously. He will desire nothing more than to quickly understand each new exercise and successfully perform it for you. This also applies to his ability to concentrate, which is increased as he learns to process instructions. The steady and swift change from one trick to the next trains his brain to focus, and the speed of his response to aids increases significantly.

Recognition of Your Work A not-to-be-underestimated aspect, which hardly anyone thinks of at first, is the recognition of achievement that you can experience through public performance. If you are confident enough to present yourself, your horse, and your "act" to others, you will receive compliments and expressions of amazement at what you have accomplished. Your family, friends, and barnmates are sure to reward you with applause. So, use a holiday celebration or a local horse show as an opportunity for a public performance, and enjoy the positive feedback!

Meeting Challenges The last great thing about tricks that I will mention specifically is simply the challenge of them. The lessons present varied demands, and it is appealing to try to surmount these challenges with your horse.

There are other benefits as well, including:

> Developing a safe and trusting interaction with your horse.
> Learning different communication techniques, which signals produce which behavior, and how to refine them.
> Using your imagination as you invent new ways of incorporating tricks into your general training regimen— and if you perform, in your attempts to surprise and amaze an audience.
> Developing good analytical skills, as not only is your end goal important; a good process for getting there is also required.

My sensitive Trakhener mare tends to be easily excitable, so the mastery of particularly challenging exercises, such as riding through the Ribbon Wall, is even more gratifying!

> The Learning Environment and Communication

I have, over the course of time, developed the following Six Phases of Training, which I feel apply to all types of horse training—whether in-hand, under saddle, or tricks:

Phase 1 When I give a signal I make certain that...
Phase 2 ...the movement to which I have assigned the signal follows, so that...
Phase 3 ...the horse understands the signal and attempts to perform the movement...
Phase 4 ...at which point he begins to "evaluate" the exercise ("This is too difficult," "This is stupid," "I don't know how to coordinate my body," and so on).
Phase 5 Now I have to make sure that the horse does not feel overwhelmed. I have to encourage him and urge him on so that he begins to accept the exercise.
Phase 6 Because of that acceptance, the exercise becomes repeatable upon request.

Six Phases of Training

Phase 1
Give signal

Phase 2
Demonstrate the movement

Phase 3
Horse understands

Phase 4
Horse decides to react favorably

Phase 5
Horse accepts

Phase 6
Exercise can be summoned on cue

The trainer must determine how best to elicit the desired movement from his or her horse. Here, Unrolling the Carpet is accomplished by hiding treats within the rolls.

At this point in my own development as a horse trainer, I no longer see the success of an exercise merely in the horse's ability to perform it, but rather in his understanding and acceptance of it. What is the difference? If your so-called "success" is limited due to the horse's lack of understanding and acceptance, then the training process must be refined accordingly. The horse should consciously decide that a given exercise is "good," not in any way overwhelming or oppressive, and that it is fun to do. If you limit your definition of "success" to merely the horse's physical ability to perform a movement, then ultimately, it is based only on a huge number of repetitions, or if the horse is not physically able to perform the exercise, then analysis as to why this is so.

Example: Atop the Mountain

In this exercise, the horse must bring his fore- and hind legs close together under his body on the small surface area provided by a raised pedestal or pallet (see more on this exercise on p. 74). Usually it takes weeks or months for a horse to master this exercise. Do you know why it requires so much time?

My Barros learned this exercise in 14 days, even though he had a weak topline. It was actually because of this that I wanted to work on this particular exercise with him. I assumed that this horse would need a lot more time than others to learn the exercise since he would first need to "get in shape" with appropriate stretching exercises. But, that was not the case.

The **Atop the Mountain** exercise requires the horse to climb upon a pedestal and bring his forelegs and hind legs close together on the small surface area. Here, Tabea and I show several of the steps.

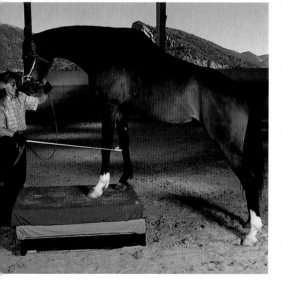
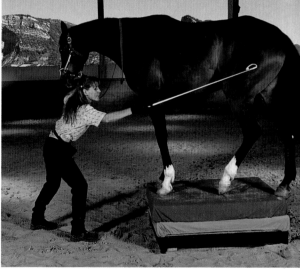

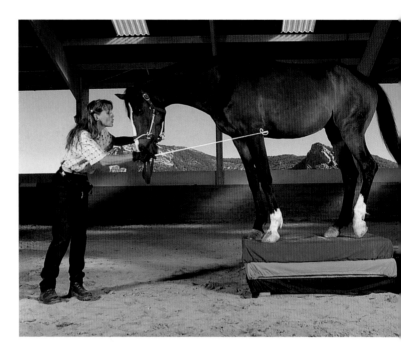

Step-by-step, Tabea climbs Atop the Mountain with vocal urging and treats. When she is situated safely, I praise her exuberantly for a job well done.

As soon as Barros realized that all he had to do to complete the trick and earn his reward was to keep his forehand in place and move his hind feet closer to his forefeet, he promptly did it without needing lengthy preparation.

This is an unbelievably important example because it demonstrates how you must make an exercise "appetizing" to your horse. You must arrange the stages or steps of learning in such a way that the horse feels neither over-challenged nor oppressed, and so he retains his trust in you as the trainer. The individual steps must each be so small that the horse says to himself, "This is a little bit difficult—but, she insists I can do it, and she demands so little of me at one time that I will manage to do it anyway." I have many other examples in which mental/emotional acceptance of an exercise was more important than the horse's physical ability to complete it. However, delving into them goes beyond the scope of this book.

In practice, tricks require specific signals to which particular movements/behaviors apply. It is the trainer's job to find a way to elicit the desired movement from the horse when the signal is given—for example, yielding, lifting a leg, stepping backward, and the like. The horse must understand what he is supposed to do. When he responds correctly, he is instantly rewarded—with both your voice and treats. He will soon be able to recognize a signal, follow it

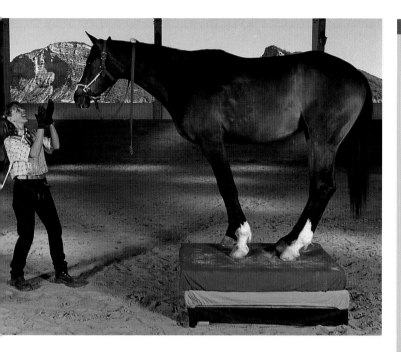

> We do not sufficiently think through a situation before making a request of our horse, but nevertheless maintain we are in the right.
> We are not aware that the "foreign-language speaker" (the horse) has not understood us.
> We communicate unclearly, but refuse to acknowledge it.
> We do not spend enough time and effort analyzing the best way to accomplish or explain an exercise or movement to our horse.

This means the same thing for riding disciplines as it does for tricks: Our methodology, our explanation, and our communication must all be so clear that the horse understands and accepts an exercise, as well as becomes physically capable of completing it.

with a required movement, and very quickly thereafter receive his food reward. The horse learns, "I receive something for my effort." He then becomes highly motivated to cooperate and accepts the exercise. So, instead of simply physically preparing horses for lessons and exercises (that is, conditioning them with trot work, stretching them with lateral work), we must concentrate on motivating them so this act of acceptance is likely. Once the horse accepts an exercise, he has confirmed that he understands it, and thus the desired movements can be performed upon request.

In behavioral science this is called positive reinforcement. Correct behavior is immediately confirmed with a reward. Negative reinforcement means to discontinue something unpleasant to the horse (say, the tap of a whip)—so correct behavior is confirmed with removal of an irritant.

The bigger your repertoire of tricks becomes over the course of time, the more quickly your horse will learn new things because of all the positive experiences he has had learning with you. Training horses with rewards works so well and easily because the horse is a herd animal, and he constantly strives to be with his own kind and other living beings by adapting himself and making himself liked so that he is not excluded from the herd.

The same training methods I use on the ground when teaching my horse tricks can also be successful when used from the saddle.

› Ramifications for Riding

I eventually began looking into whether the same training procedures I use for teaching horses tricks could be carried over into ridden work, driving, longeing, and other work in-hand. In my mind, riding is the most exacting of all these activities, but for the horse I feel it is by far the most frustrating and boring one.

So, if we were to apply my six-phase training system in the riding arena, wouldn't it be necessary to immediately confirm ridden training with rewards? Just as with tricks, the horse is conditioned to respond to signals—in this case, the rider's aids. I feel that if you divide a ridden lesson into short, easily understood steps, and communicate to the horse which sequence of movements you want from a specific signal, when the horse performs correctly he should be promptly rewarded with a treat.

Does this mean that every time my horse executes a nice round circle I should stop, give him a treat, and say "Super!"? The idea of it probably seems outlandish, but—strictly speaking—this is how my methods should be interpreted. Does it seem silly to you?

Remember, when training tricks you do this constantly: signal » performance » reward. In your daily ridden work you have the opportunity to do the same thing—enrich schooling sessions with regular feedback, including your voice, strokes, and pats. Pause long enough after new or especially challenging exercises to give your horse a food reward. Even a short rest break (without food) can be enough reward for the horse.

If you do this consistently, the horse will recognize that it was not just any random movement that he just performed, but a specific one, and that he did his part well. Because of your use of positive reinforcement, the horse becomes more intensively involved in his training. He is no longer a voiceless robot that performs serpentines, lead changes, circles, and the like, one after the other.

What I would like to do is help all of your training and riding become a more joyful, cheerful, and encouraging experience—for both you and your horse. I am absolutely certain that this is possible. The first step is to recognize that it is okay to use verbal or tactile praise during ridden work. I personally have absolutely no qualms about dismounting and happily showering my horse with abundant praise, feeding him treats, and petting him after an extraordinary performance of a movement he has long found difficult. I always convey my joy at a successful breakthrough with great effusiveness. I then remount and we get back to work, both the better for the moment of celebration. And why not? I understand that this might not be everyone's cup of tea, but I do encourage you to find your own balance between "depressing" ring work with little or no feedback, and my own exuberantly effusive way.

There is one point to consider: It is much easier to give enthusiastic and encouraging praise from the ground where you are on the same plane and in the same field of vision as the horse. Even I often become mute while riding. Why is that? It is probably at least partly because when riding we must concentrate on the complex challenges we face in the saddle, checking numerous details of our own position as well as that of the horse. Most people become silent when they concentrate on technique, body control, and the horse's movement. In the midst of this effort, it is difficult to remain in verbal contact with the horse.

As soon as you take a moment to praise your horse, you may feel that you lose your focus on yourself, necessary corrections to your position may be omitted, or you feel disconnected from your body. Keep practicing! You will soon master your work so well that you will find it easier to "take up voice contact" with your horse. (If you are already able to verbally praise your horse while doing work that requires concentration, hats off to you! Carry on.)

Of course, none of what I've discussed takes into account the fact that the riding environment often neither desires nor permits verbal contact with the horse. Old cavalry rules come into play, such as: "One should not babble on in the arena like a waterfall," "The horse should obey the rider's aids," "The horse will be distracted," "Chatter disturbs the other riders," and so on.

I communicate constantly with my horse when riding, using my voice, strokes, and pats to praise him for work well done.

Riding Example: The Volte The following errors, among others, can occur while executing a volte (a small circle with a diameter of 6, 8, or 10 meters) on horseback. The horse:

> is too slow or too fast.
> leans on the outside shoulder and "falls out."
> leans on his inside shoulder and "falls in."
> allows his hindquarters to fall in or fall out. (In other words, he is not able to remain "straight" through the body while traveling on a curved line.)
> has an incorrect head or neck position—for example, he is on the forehand or behind the bit.

First, you must analyze the problem and break it down into its components. Then you can clarify each detail separately for your horse, just as you would when training him a trick.

Too Slow If the horse goes too slowly, ride him out of the volte and onto a straight line. As his body loses the bend necessary to travel a circular figure, the horse will accelerate. Give him the reins and, employing the appropriate voice, leg, and whip aids, establish the

If you have a specific under-saddle problem, analyze it, and then work on each detail individually—for example, bending (1), stretching (2), and lengthening (3) may all be necessary to improve your horse's voltes or circles, and each should get separate attention.

tempo (the speed of repetition of strides) you want. When the horse maintains the faster tempo with even rhythm, go back to the volte without shortening the reins, and maintain it with voice, leg, and whip. As soon as your horse does this correctly, "go large" (ride around the whole arena), then shorten the reins again. If your horse interprets this as a signal to reduce speed, loosen the rein contact and use the driving aids until the tempo is once again correct. Before you again shorten the reins, drive energetically with the whip. Then immediately take up the reins.

Repeat this sequence until your horse has grasped the idea that taking up the reins or direct contact with his mouth is not the same as "slow down." When your horse has dealt with this issue successfully, give him praise, praise, praise! Continue riding around the whole arena with your horse maintaining the tempo while you take up (or shorten) the reins and lengthen them again, by turns. No matter what length of rein you have, your horse should maintain the desired tempo. Keep your legs very still. If your horse slows down again, remind him with brief, emphatic use of the whip aid, then praise him immediately when he responds correctly.

When your horse completes the exercise successfully on a straight line, ride large circles and demand he keep the same

tempo. Praise him. Progressively bring the size of the circles down to the size of a volte, which by this time should no longer be associated with slowing down. Remember to praise your horse at every successful intermediate step!

Too Fast A different procedure is used for a horse that speeds up in the volte. Remain in the volte because the repeated tight turns can help you decrease the tempo. If, despite that, the horse does not travel in a more relaxed fashion, try some stretching and head-lowering exercises, such as the kind you use to relax the horse as you warm up.

Falls Out with the Shoulder When the horse "falls out" in the volte, the cause, naturally, is his crookedness. No young and untrained horse is totally straight, but rather is "hollow" on the right or left side. If the horse is hollow to the left, for example, he will automatically shift his weight to the right shoulder. The result is he enlarges the volte with every step when traveling on the left rein (to the left).

You must counteract this tendency with appropriate exercises. Ride a large circle on the left rein and decrease its size until it is a volte. As you do so, position your horse to the outside: Slightly

In every riding discipline, the rider must analyze whether her horse's head/neck carriage is appropriate and whether the connection from the horse's mouth to her hands is sufficiently light.

shorten the right rein and, at the same time, slightly lengthen the left rein. The horse's head is now positioned to the right while he travels left with his shoulders. Support this movement by shifting your weight to the left and using a driving aid at the girth on the right side or a whip aid on the right shoulder. (You may first have to clarify for your horse what the tap of the whip on the shoulder means, and this is best accomplished through work on the ground.) When you are able to, "give" the right rein to the horse. Repeat this exercise many times, and do not forget to praise him after each attempt! After many repetitions, you will be able to bend the horse to the inside of the volte without having him "drift away."

Falls In with the Shoulder This tendency, too, is caused by the horse's crookedness. Let us again refer to our example of a horse that is hollow to the left—he "falls in" on the shoulder in a volte on the right rein because his balance is on the right shoulder and his body follows his stronger right side (to the inside). So, in this direction the horse must learn to enlarge the volte.

Position the horse with his head to the right (to the inside of the volte), shift your weight to the left, and drive the horse to the left with your right leg (or a signal with the whip on his right shoulder—remember the horse might first best learn to yield to the touch of the whip on his right shoulder from the ground). Move both hands to the left. This influences the shoulders and your horse will drift left onto a bigger circle. Praise every small success.

Practice this as often as possible until you can ride your horse in a uniform volte with an inside bend.

Another method of dealing with this problem on the same rein (and one that is easier for the horse) is to gradually enlarge a square figure. Practice this many times with your horse bent strongly to the right (the inside of the square). You will notice that he becomes "soft," and you can soon move from a square shape to the circle in the exercise just described. Make it a rule that whenever you ride on the right rein, you enlarge the pattern you are riding.

Always divide ridden exercises into many small steps—as you will do with tricks—and praise lavishly. Your horse will be grateful that you express yourself clearly and reward his progress.

Falls Out or In with the Hindquarters When your horse is not straight through his body on a curved line, lateral movements such as shoulder-in and haunches-in will correct the problem.

On the Forehand or Heavy in the Hands Counter this issue by coming to a square halt and raising the horse's neck with bit pressure (raise both hands) so that he leans less on his shoulders, and therefore is also less "heavy in your hands." Take this exercise a step further by shifting his weight backward. While the horse is standing still, mobilize his jaws by flexing him to the left and to the right, and encourage him to "release" and stretch his neck forward. If the horse again begins to lean on your hands, repeat this exercise. Many horses are heavy in the hands because they are searching for balance. Shifting their weight backward helps them find it.

Above or Behind the Bit This problem is again remedied by mobilizing the jaw and flexing the horse to each side. It is frequently the rider's lack of experience that leads to this issue, as early symptoms of the problem aren't recognized and addressed immediately. Ignorance and lack of attention sadly lead to many misunderstandings, often to the horse's detriment.

These examples demonstrate how you have to analyze a lesson and the problems you may have with it, then break the issue down into individual problem areas for the horse to focus on and understand. As you do this, mistakes are gradually eliminated, and if, along the way, every bit of progress is acknowledged with praise, the horse becomes aware of the right way to perform a movement and so overall improvement is certain.

To improve my own ridden work, I adhere to the very effective recommendations of my husband, Philippe Karl, whose many books provide valuable insights into work in-hand and under saddle, and in my opinion are indispensable texts on classical equitation and horse training.

When you have a horse that tends to go "heavy in your hands" or "behind the bit," you need to get his weight off his forehand (in the first scenario) "open up" his neck (in the second). Begin by raising both hands.

The pressure on the reins causes the horse to yield his lower jaw.

Next, flex your horse from side-to-side (here, to the left) to encourage him to stretch forward with his neck.

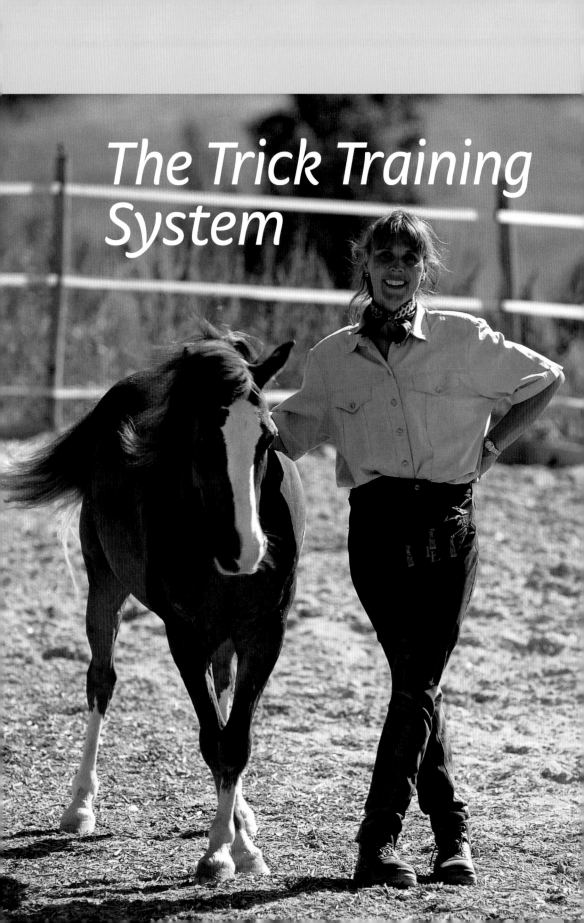

The Trick Training System

› Atmosphere

The first element important in trick training is *atmosphere*, which should be thoroughly positive throughout—that is, supportive and encouraging. It is your job as the trainer to establish a positive tone, approach the work with both foresight and a sense of fun, and by emanating encouragement, inspire your horse to willingly participate. Horses are sensitive to mood and tone, so begin each new exercise with confidence, plan the progression of your training, and end the session when your horse has performed an assignment well.

› Verbal Praise

Verbal praise is instantaneous voice feedback to a response from the horse. It is used when both your hands are involved in an exercise and you cannot reward with stroking or reach for a treat. With verbal praise or words that are confirming or encouraging, you can also support the horse's attempts that may tend in the right direction: "Good," "Yes, that's right," "Fine, yes"—the words can be anything you please as long as your tone of voice is always friendly. If you want to praise an attempt or accomplishment particularly intensely, make your voice even friendlier, more enthusiastic, and pitch it slightly higher.

Important note: In order for the horse to make the necessary connection, *every* reward, including verbal praise, should be given *within seven seconds* of the horse giving the desired response. This narrow window of time has been confirmed in practice through the method of trial and error.

I believe in rewarding a particularly good performance with friendly applause.

Horses recognize friendly gestures and speech.

› "Hands-On" Praise

When your hands are free, reward the horse with strokes when he has done a movement correctly. "Hands-on" praise ranges from a gentle to firm stroking of the neck or head. There are actually few horses that appreciate the hard "pats" and "slaps" on the neck, chest, or croup that a great many people use as a "reward."

Many horses do not like being touched around the head, so hands-on praise should not include the head until the horse has, through gentle touching elsewhere on his body, acquired a liking for it. Linda Tellington-Jones' TTouches are very good for building trust in this area, and in others (see p. xiii).

Hands-on praise is an enhancement of verbal praise and should be given during a short pause after a horse has performed an exercise well.

I reserve generous amounts of stroking and scratching as a reward for desired movements or behavior.

> Food Rewards

Like the other forms of reward, treats must be given quickly following an exercise done well in order for the horse to directly link the two. Therefore, you should already have the treat in your hand when you are preparing to ask for a movement. As noted at the beginning of the book, a hip pouch (fanny pack) is useful and lets you avoid time-consuming searches in pant or jacket pockets. (I discussed various types of appropriate food rewards on p. 7.)

With respect to this type of reward, it is very important to be disciplined in your approach, since many people are averse to giving treats because they fear their horses will get greedy and begin to beg.

After an obedient halt without a bridle or reins, Tabea promptly gets a food reward.

Feeding Discipline You cannot help but increase the horse's motivation to perform with food. However, *feeding discipline* is an unbelievably important matter when using food rewards. The horse should not become restless in anticipation of a treat, nor should the horse lose his concentration or develop bad habits because of it. Such behavior would not only undermine the training process, it would leave you frustrated and unsafe, as well.

The most important rule is this: The time and place for giving a treat are always determined by *you*. Establish this lesson before using food rewards in your training regimen.

Stand next to the horse with about 5 feet between you, and direct his head away from you with the help of the handle-end of a dressage whip. Rustle around in your fanny pack, open it, and provoke the horse into coming toward you. When he does, immediately make it clear to him with a whip signal that this is *not* desired. Opening the fanny pack and/or rummaging around in it should not be misconstrued by the horse as a signal to come to you and beg for food.

If the horse begins to paw, come closer and stoke his legs with the whip to quiet him. If that does not work, admonish him with a stern voice command, such as "Whoa!" or "No!" Touching his chest with the whip may also help. As he calms, reinforce the behavior with stroking and quiet talk. If the horse stops pawing, praise him. Then, distance yourself from him again, raise the whip, and vibrate it quickly from side to side between you, about 4 inches from the horse's head.

Now, to show the horse how to properly receive a treat, place yourself on the horse's left side with the lead rope in your left hand and the whip in your right. Lower the whip and step closer to the horse (remember, the horse can never approach you for his treat). With your hand very low, offer the horse a treat on the *right* side of his head so that he has to turn away from you to take it. To do this, reach under the horse's neck with the treat in your *right* hand so that your hand is next to the right side of the horse's mouth. (Remain on the horse's left side while doing this.)

Once the horse takes the treat, step away from him back to your normal "working distance." At this point your horse will likely turn his head toward you and may even begin to walk in your direction. This should be discouraged by again lifting the whip and vigorously moving it from side to side between you, indicating to your horse he should not follow you, either with his head or his whole body.

Practice feeding discipline by repeating this exercise many times. As you do so, learn to be precise and deliberate in your actions.

When teaching feeding discipline, hold the handle end of a dressage whip between you and your horse to maintain the appropriate distance.

Rummage around in your fanny pack—this will likely provoke the horse into turning his head and/or coming closer to you.

When this happens, correct your horse, using the handle-end of the whip again to maintain the desired distance.

The horse must learn: "I will not be rewarded with treats when I move closer to my trainer, and I must not ask for food. When I move without being asked or I beg for food, I am only told to halt or stand still." There will, of course, be some horses that do not behave sensibly where food is concerned. For your own safety, these individuals must be told very strictly what is permitted and what is not.

Even when there is a greater distance between the horse and trainer, a whip can still be used effectively to indicate the appropriate space between horse and handler.

› Pausing

The *pause*—or a short rest between instructions—is another effective training tool. During a pause the horse can think about the exercise he just completed. A short rest is interpreted by him as positive feedback. When pausing, you should simply let the horse stand peacefully while you stay a sufficient distance away and do not communicate with him.

Ben and I pause frequently between exercises. One of us thinks, while the other rests.

› Ignoring

If your horse does something that bothers or annoys you, or that does not serve the purpose of the exercise, simply *ignore* the action and continue giving the cue or signal for the desired behavior or movement. The horse learns that one action (the wrong behavior) gets no response and no reward, whereas a different action (the right behavior) gets both response and reward.

› Punishment

Punishment should be used only when a horse deliberately and consciously disobeys you, even after you have explained to him several times what it is you want. In addition, you must be absolutely certain that your explanations of the exercise were indeed understood. So, for example, if your horse refuses to stand still, or if he totally ignores you and moves past you after several repetitions of the command "Whoa!" (the meaning of which he has long known), you have the right to forcefully stop him by emphatically stepping into his path and clearly bringing the whip to his chest, and if necessary, by also touching him with the whip.

Just as precise timing plays a crucial role in rewarding the horse, so does it in the act of punishment. It is very important to react precisely "on the spot" with the correction of misbehavior. Do not forget to praise the obedience that follows the correction, and use praise to the same degree as you did punishment—after a harsh punishment, obedience is generously rewarded, and after a minor bit of disciplining, some friendly praise follows.

Ben demonstrates his "displeasure" on cue.

› Duration and Intensity of Training

You can use tricks as stand-alone training sessions, but they also combine well with other types of work. For example, you might begin a riding session with the Spanish Walk, and maybe end with a Bow or Sitting Down.

To make good, steady progress you should practice tricks four or five times a week. Your repertoire will constantly expand and the variation of your work will steadily increase. This means you will eventually need more time to devote to trick training, if that is what you would like to focus on with your horse. With Ben, for example, I have difficulty keeping all the movements that he knows fresh in his mind. Ideally, I would work with him twice a day, but I seldom manage to do that, as I'm sure you can imagine!

As a rule an exercise should not be repeated too frequently. This is something that you learn very quickly and clearly from trick training. Too many repetitions can send you in the opposite direction from where you want to go, and you may experience the quality of tricks steadily deteriorating. In general, when training horses it is best to limit the number of attempts you make to get a horse to do something. This way you remain effective—your horse does not become frustrated or bored because of your "doggedness."

When you limit the number of repetitions from the outset, you must consider beforehand exactly which steps you will need to have mastered in order to advance in your next attempt. Naturally, it makes sense to always end a session during a good moment. Keep in mind that because you reward even the smallest advances in the learning process, your training should always end on a positive note.

The number of attempts you make should also suit your horse. Observe whether repetitions improve your horse's performance or deteriorate it. Over the course of time and training your horse will let you know how many repetitions of the various exercises he will tolerate.

One explanation for why I find only minimal repetitions necessary—even with my new horses like Tabea and Anouk—lies in the positive work atmosphere I believe is so important to training. My horses are visibly happy when we work together.

› Commands

Always use the same commands for specific exercises. I recommend creating a list and writing it down so you can keep your voice commands straight. These combine with your tone of voice, body language and movement, as well as with "touch" signals from your whip or hands. However, the voice commands, above all, must be employed very precisely.

Within a herd, horses employ nonverbal communication almost exclusively. This explains why the voice plays a subordinate role to visual commands during training. Horses get their first information from touch. The type of touch used must depend on the sensitivity of the individual horse. During early stages of training, the touch cue must be so persistent that the horse notices it and is influenced by it. Later, your horse will orient himself to your posture and movement, rather than just the touch. It can be days, or even weeks, after an exercise *is first executed* successfully through body language or a touch of the whip, before it is finally associated with and confirmed by a verbal command. For this reason alone it is important to always use the same voice command—words, pitch, and intonation—so not to confuse the horse.

It is helpful if you first familiarize yourself with the commands that seem to be logically connected to specific exercises and already fall *easily* from your own lips. When you begin training you will see how challenging it is, with our extensive vocabulary, to use only your deliberately chosen commands and not overwhelm the horse with multiple instructions for the same action. However, with time, you will continually improve.

"Alley Oop!" is the verbal command I use for the rear. My body language and the movement of the whip reinforce Ben's understanding of the voice command.

Examples of Vocal Commands

Command	Effect
"And walk!"	Upward transition to walk
"And trot!"	Upward transition to trot
"And can-*ter!*"	Upward transition to canter
"*Whoa*, halt..."	Halt and stand
"*Whoa, wa*-alk..."	Downward transition to walk
"*Whoa, tr*-rot..."	Downward transition to trot
"Whoa in walk"	Slow the walk
"Whoa in trot"	Slow the trot
"Whoa in canter"	Slow the canter
"Bo-*ow*"	Kneel on one knee, one foreleg outstretched
"Plié"	Lower the chest with forelegs outstretched
"Kneel"	Kneel on both knees
"*Come* here"	Come to me
"And cha-*ange*"	Change direction
"Tu-*rn*"	Turn in a circle
"Ba-*ack*," or "Back up"	Step backward
"*No*"	Negates the undesired action

Note: The *italicized* syllables should be emphasized and stretched out.

› Saying "No"

With my method of training I basically tell the horse what he *should* do. I very seldom use the word "No" because it does not help create clarity. Although "No" can stop the horse in the process of executing a movement, he is left in the dark as to what he should do instead. I find it is better to simply repeat what it is he *should* do in a more *admonishing* way. For example, if the horse is supposed to give you his hoof and instead sinks down to bow on one knee, say "Foot!" again more firmly, rather than saying "No," and again repeat the command.

› Differentiating between Exercises

When you shift from one lesson to the next, it is important to always consider whether you have sufficiently differentiated the cues for each exercise, and whether the situation is clear enough for the horse to understand. Many exercises are only slightly different from the next, and yet we expect the horse to distinguish between them. Put yourself in his place—he does not speak the language, has totally different needs, and communicates in an entirely different way than you.

› The "On" and "Off" Switches

By the "on" and "off" switches I mean that a particular exercise is to be performed when a certain signal/command is given, and it should end with another signal/command, or with a reward. The horse must perform an exercise only when I ask for it, and only as many times as I ask for it.

Ben and I discuss saddling techniques.

Let's look at the example of the Spanish Walk. When my horse knows the exercise well and has learned that he gets praise and treats for lifting and stretching his forelegs forward in an exaggerated manner as he walks, he may begin to lift and stretch his legs of his own volition, without being asked (this can particularly happen with very enthusiastic horses). I accept this behavior in the first or second training session so that I do not discourage the horse (see An Exception, p. 34), but thereafter, I react to the Spanish Walk *only* when it follows my command for it. Otherwise, I ignore the horse or reprimand him.

It is important to practice in advance the stop signal ("Whoa, halt") so that undesired performances can be nipped in the bud. The "off" button—the ability to end an exercise at any point—is nearly as important as the ability to call it up at any time. If an undesired exercise cannot be terminated or blocked you will likely grow frustrated when you want to build on what the horse has already learned.

When they want to avoid another command or when they are bored with the training process, horses often like to perform, unbidden, exercises that they know well. You can block such misbehavior by halting the horse, having him back up, or asking him to step forward. The reflex to block unwanted exercises with specific counteractions like these must become automatic for you. Thus, the "Whoa, halt" command has great significance because most of the time I end a trick with that cue. "No" can be used as a command with overtones of punishment, whereas "Whoa, halt" signals a positive conclusion to an exercise. I also use the command "Walk on" to end an exercise like the Spanish Walk, for example, or to block an undesired Bow by physically raising the horse's head and sending him forward so he loses his focus on the incorrect exercise.

Once you have mastered many trick routines, you may get a little overconfident and lazy, and give the horse imprecise commands. This leads to sloppy performance and undesired behavior. Be particularly strict with yourself as you and your horse progress. Your leadership qualities develop here as you make sure you deliver clear instructions that your horse can interpret and perform precisely.

An Exception There is an exception to the "on/off" rule: You may allow your horse to perform exercises that you have not requested if they are ones he has not yet mastered or he performs only reluctantly. In these cases, do not block or punish the performance or exercise if he offers it. For example, if you are working on the Spanish Walk and your horse does not yet know which touch command indicates the movement, he may not lift his foreleg when asked. Then, perhaps he *finally* stretches his leg forward—but without being cued to do so! At this point, praise him! You need to make it clear to him that what he has done is indeed a movement you want.

At the beginning of learning a new lesson I always allow a short phase when the horse can, without reprimand, demonstrate the new trick without having first been given the appropriate command. This phase might only last the length of the first training session, or if the exercise has been extraordinarily difficult for the horse to learn or entailed overcoming many "challenges," it might last for days. When the horse indicates that he understands the trick and performs it gladly, then I increase the difficulty by explaining he may only perform the exercise on command.

As another example, let's look at Ben's "Pointing Pirouette" (a pirouette with one foreleg extended out in front of him). At first,

More challenging tricks, such as this one with all four of Ben's feet off the ground, require the trainer to possess strong leadership qualities and expertise.

Ben could lift a foreleg, stretch it out, and hold it there in the air. In order to increase his motivation to perform the entire exercise, I allowed him to demonstrate this part of the trick whenever he wanted. The same thing when we added the pirouette. I wanted to really encourage him because the exercise is a difficult one. Today he can do it all by himself, and even without me standing beside him.

In another example, Ben can rear in an entirely safe way (he does not use rearing to "attack" me). So when we are working together, I allow him to rear at anytime. Increasing his motivation to do so makes it easier for me to develop the Courbette (a series of multiple "jumps" on the hind legs) or teach Ben to walk on his hind legs.

Making exceptions to strict rules is something reserved for experienced trainers, who always do so fully aware of their horses' behaviors and the boundaries that should not be crossed.

As a bit of an aside: I feel it is important that in the beginning stages of trick training other people are not allowed to work with your horse. Also, if it can be helped, routine farrier and veterinarian visits should be scheduled for weeks later in the training process, once your methods of communicating with your horse have been confirmed.

› Which Tricks to Teach?

There are probably certain tricks that you already know you absolutely want to teach your horse and some that you do not want to do at all. On the one hand, this is a matter of taste, but on the other, it is also a question of whether or not you want to integrate certain behaviors into your horse's repertoire. In the end, an individual horse's self-confidence, obedience, and/or tendency toward dominance play a crucial role in your consideration of which tricks to teach.

A typical example is the trick Saying "Yes" and "No." Once a horse has learned this exercise, he may form a tendency to offer it without being asked because he thinks it is the simplest way to get treats. If it will bother you when your horse greets you this way, or if he is likely to stand in his stall continually Saying "Yes" or "No" in an attempt to entice food treats from passers-by, then you should definitely not teach him this trick.

Now consider the Spanish Walk—you should be aware of the dangers related to a sudden, unbidden display of this trick. Depending on how large your horse is, an unexpectedly outstretched leg can cause injury even when working in quite a large area. In addition, the Nudging trick can lead to undesired situations. My pony, Ben, may "push" me from behind on command—but this is acceptable primarily because of his small size. I do not think I would necessarily teach this trick to a large horse.

Be sure to consider which tricks make sense if children or multiple people handle your horse. Safety should be a primary concern and could greatly limit your repertoire.

A trick's "on" and "off" switches must be firmly ingrained in the foundation of the horse's understanding of the exercise, and easily employed by the trainer at a moment's notice. The Spanish Walk, shown here, is a trick horses are particularly prone to offering without a cue to do so.

› From Starting Point to End Goal

In order to recognize and separate "building blocks" or individual learning steps, you must have an image of both your *starting point* and your *end goal*. Let us take the example of Backing-Up. Your starting point is a horse that can, in a halter and on a short lead rope, be directed backward. Your image of the end goal is a picture of your horse walking backward through a slalom made of five barrels, at liberty, with you behind him.

Beginning from this starting point, and with this goal in mind, you need to employ as many intermediate steps as is necessary for the horse to understand and accept the exercise (see p. 38). Consider carefully the purpose of each step, and create a list or make sketches to illustrate them. (You will find how-to instructions for backing-up on p. 50.)

Here I work with Ben on one intermediate stage (or "building block") on the path from starting point (Backing-Up in-hand with whip and lead cues) to end goal (Backing-Up at liberty).

Here you can see another inter-mediate stage in the Backing-Up exercise. I am still cuing Ben from the front, although now without a halter and lead. Eventually, I hope to be able to perform this trick by cueing Ben from behind.

Using this "starting point to end goal" method, you can proceed sensibly and successfully with your training. It can also be carried directly over to your work under saddle: Overly aggressive moments occur when the rider, with her goal in mind but with demanding, too strong aids, "breaks into the house without knocking." In other words the rider has not analyzed the construction and development of the lesson, and so has not identified the individual intermediate steps necessary to its successful completion. She simply proceeds with an image of her end goal. Trot lengthenings, for example, are often forced without it having been made clear to the horse what it is the rider wants, and without having first established the correct head and neck position that allows forward-reaching, ground-covering strides. The inevitable result is a tense and unhappy horse.

› Making Connections

A very significant aspect of training is to establish connections. This means that a long-practiced, well-done, confirmed stage of learning is connected with a new one, so that you are always progressing to new movement from an old one. By correctly executing the old familiar exercise, the horse gains the necessary motivation and self-confidence to approach a new challenge.

Let me break this down for you with an example. Let's say your horse is "up in the bridle" and "on the bit," and you would like to change his head and neck position into a stretch that reaches forward and down:

Step 1 Stand on the ground and flex your horse laterally. This signal tells him to drop his head.

Step 2 The next time you ride, ask for the same flexion at the halt. If your horse does not understand you, dismount and ask for the flexion from the ground again (you are connecting Step 1 to Step 2).

Step 3 Next, let the horse move into the walk, and give the signal to flex while he is in motion. If he does not understand, halt and ask for it while he is standing still (connecting Step 2 to Step 3). Then, try again at a walk. Return to the halt as often as you need to until your horse understands what he is supposed to do.

Remember: Whenever your horse has understood an interim step, praise him generously!

› Going Back a Step or Two

When your horse does not understand something, don't hesitate to go one step back in the training sequence. If you have already worked on higher level exercises and your horse regresses in the work on a bad day, go back as far as necessary for you and your horse to find the tiniest bit of common ground. It is only by doing this that you will have a chance to finish the training session on a positive note.

Practice patience and self-discipline, and in your work with your horse, always be prepared to "come down off of your high horse." We have a natural inclination and desire "to be right," both with other humans and with horses. We need to mold this into a "readiness-to-understand." If you think your horse is taking advantage of you or intentionally misbehaving, go back a few steps! Only when you have consistently and correctly worked on a particular movement do you have the right to be a bit stricter—assuming that the horse has done the movement obediently in the past. Unfortunately, horses cannot speak and let us know what ails them. You cannot feel what your horse feels. Tomorrow, he could be in a better mood and your performance could go perfectly again.

An example of how one stage of a lesson, done correctly, should "connect" with the next, more difficult stage: When I flex my horse to the left from the ground (1), he reaches into the stretch (2). The work on the ground should "connect" to the next stage of the lesson in the saddle—flexing and stretching at the halt (3).

Reviving the Riding Horse with Trick Training Methodology

> The Basic Course for Riders

As I have already mentioned, I am of the opinion that many horses suffer from, are bored by—or, at best, enjoy very little—their ridden work. Therefore, it is my intention that this book helps make clear how easily any riding discipline can be brightened with an injection of light and joyful spirit.

Wouldn't you like your horse to gladly and enthusiastically work with you every time you ride from now on? If your answer is "Yes!" you and your horse should undertake a two-week retraining program. During the first week you will do nothing but my suggested tricks. In the second week you will critically observe everything you do on and around your horse and incorporate clear communication and a rewards system every step along the way. And from the third week on, you will integrate these new ideas into your regular riding program.

As mentioned earlier, I would like you to learn to reward your horse for every little success with treats. Your horse should understand that from this day forward it pays to:

> do things correctly.
> think along with you.
> concentrate.

because he profits in the form of:

> verbal praise.
> "hands-on" praise—stroking, petting.
> food rewards—promised and guaranteed.

You must discover a way to have fun, even when you are working on serious under-saddle exercises.

Suggested Exercise	Number of Repetitions
1 Feeding discipline	1 time per training (see p. 27)
2 Walking forward on cue and halting on cue	10 times
3 Halting on cue and Backing-Up	10 times
4 Turning on the forehand (yielding the haunches)	5 times
5 Turning on the haunches (yielding the forehand)	5 times
6 Stepping over a pole on the ground first with one foot, then two, then three, and then four	5 times
7 Putting a foot in a car tire/wheel	5 times
8 Placing the forefeet on a doormat or piece of carpet	5 times
9 Moving a leg when it is tapped with the whip	5 times
10 Lowering the head when asked by a gentle tug on the halter	5 times
11 Giving the hoof when asked with a tap on the leg	5 times

I suggest a retraining program consisting of 11 easy in-hand exercises (see chart, p. 42).

All the exercises I recommend in the chart on p. 42 have one thing in common: Once each is completed, the horse should stand stock still while you reward him with words, your hands, and treats. Proceed according to the following rule: In exercises 2 through 5 your horse should halt after three or four steps and then you can reward him. For exercises 6 through 11, your horse should perform the exercise once, and then you should reward him before you repeat it.

For one whole week do not do anything else. Do not work your horse in any other way—no riding, no longeing, no round-penning—only work on the suggested exercises. This week is your opportunity to learn how to break the exercises down into the smallest incremental steps possible and to enthusiastically praise your horse for the tiniest accomplishment. You cannot wait until your horse accomplishes something extremely difficult—say a dressage piaffe or reining spin—to praise him for the first time! Unlike us, horses do not see one maneuver as being more valuable than another.

When you start the second week, critically observe everything you do on and around your horse. Do you consistently give your horse clear instructions for each thing that he is to do, and do you praise him when he responds correctly? Let's go over how time with your horse should look: You come into the barn, open your horse's stall door, and after a friendly greeting, halter him. Once his halter is on he should no longer be nuzzling you, but rather, patiently waiting. To ensure this, you move his head away from you and say, "Whoa, halt." When he is standing quietly you tell him, "Walk on," and walk with him into the barn aisle. There you again say, "Whoa, halt," and come to a stop. Each time he does something correctly, you reward your horse in all the possible ways (voice, hands, and food). You cross-tie him and ask him to move his hindquarters over. The horse obeys—praise! After grooming him and tacking him up, you proceed to the riding arena with everything done on your command and with you providing the appropriate feedback. You complete the day's exercises and afterward, always with clear signals, you lead your horse back into his stall, pausing every so often with "Whoa, halt," and a food reward.

After two weeks, return to your usual riding program. Everything, and I mean each and every thing—halting, standing still to be mounted, waiting to walk on, turning, and so on—should be clearly requested, and when obediently done, excessively rewarded. If you conscientiously followed the retraining program

Even just a single ground pole offers the trainer many different exercise options.

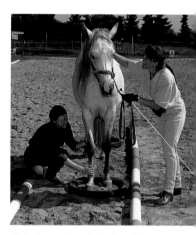

If the horse doesn't feel confident enough to stand with his feet within a tire on his own, then you can help him feel more secure with verbal and "hands-on" praise.

Whether in a halter or a bridle, the horse should learn to lower his head when asked with a gentle tug.

Riding with a only a neck ring instead of a bridle promotes a willing and contented riding partner (see my recommendations for instructions from Linda Tellington-Jones on working with the neck ring on p. xiii).

in the two weeks prior, you should notice a clear difference in your horse's behavior.

You may think that this method is way "over the top," and that it is a total exaggeration to praise and reward so much—with food, no less! You may wonder, "How long can this go on?" First of all, it

Recommended Reward Pyramid

"Super-Jackpot" Reward
Verbal praise, hands, and treats

For all "breakthroughs," or accomplishments involving courage, self-discipline, and effort.

"Excellent" Reward
Verbal praise or hands and treats, and maybe a break/pause (see p. 28).

For good performance of a current work in progress.

"Ordinary" Reward
Verbal praise (for example, "Good boy").

For all expected correct responses, such as exercises that have long been mastered and performed obediently.

Challenging situations, such as riding bridleless through a "scary" Ribbon Wall, offer the opportunity for horse and rider to develop new skills, more confidence, and happiness in each other's company, even when working under saddle.

is not "over the top" to feed a lot of treats, because no horse in the world asks to be trained, especially in highly competitive and often demanding disciplines such as those we see in the horse industry today. Second, after the retraining phase is over, you will vary how you proceed with reward-giving.

Starting today, try to work with your horse in such a way that your joy in and with each other continually increases. Good luck to you, and welcome to the International Club of Happy Riders!

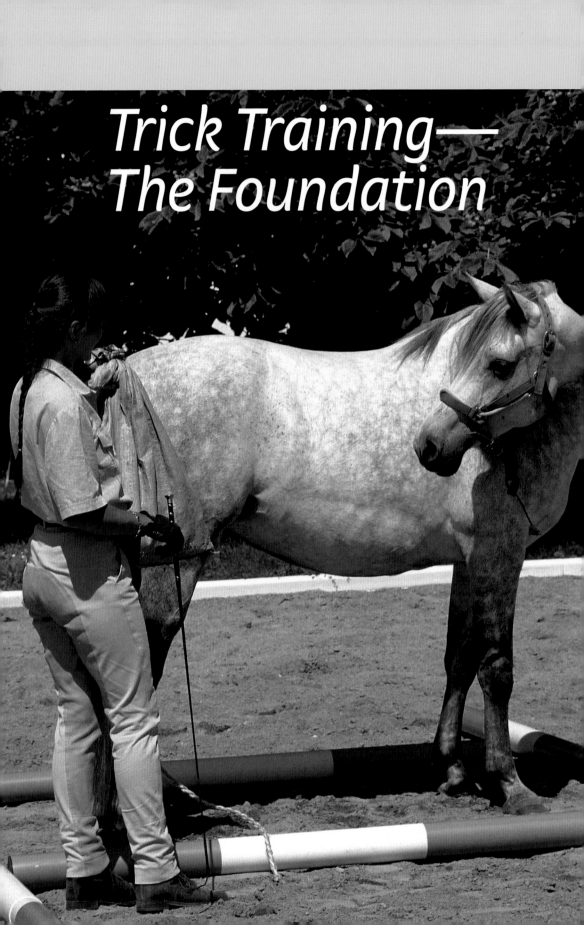

Trick Training—
The Foundation

› Basic Exercises

I have already described the prerequisites that a horse must bring to the practice ring when preparing to teach him tricks (see p. 4). As a reminder and to build upon what I've already mentioned, if you want to begin trick training immediately, your horse:

> › can be touched everywhere on his body.
> › can be led from various positions.
> › comes to a halt when asked.
> › stands calmly, both in-hand and at liberty.
> › steps backward in-hand when asked.
> › steps sideways in-hand when asked.

All these basics are very important when incorporating tricks in your training program. On the following pages, I describe the steps for teaching your horse the Statue (stands stock still when asked, until cued to move), as well as Backing-Up and Stepping Sideways.

Note: Under the "In Brief" summary of each exercise there is an instruction called "To End the Exercise." What does this mean? Remember my discussion of the "on" and "off" switches on p. 33? You not only want to be able to summon a trick upon request—you also need to have a means to "block" or end it, should your horse (without being asked) drop down into a deep bow, walk backward, or give you a friendly "push."

The Statue

The Statue is a lesson in which the horse learns to stand, at liberty, in various situations without a handler nearby. In mastering this, your horse also learns to be led, to halt, and to accept the touch of the whip all over his body.

It is best that you practice this exercise in an enclosed indoor or outdoor arena, and you should hold the lead in such a way that if the

horse should suddenly pull back, the lead can slide out of your hands without wrenching or burning your fingers.

The Statue is the most important preparatory lesson for many other tricks. To be able to trust your horse to remain in a set position brings great peace of mind to all your trick work.

1 Arrange four poles in a rectangle on the ground. The rectangle should be at least 20 inches longer and wider than the horse. Lead the horse into the rectangle, and while he stands next to you, stroke his forelegs from top to bottom with your whip—this helps "ground" the horse on the spot. Praise your horse verbally and stroke him with the whip when he stands quietly. After a minute, lead him out of the rectangle. In the future, strok-

One of my "foundation" exercises—the Statue—becomes more challenging when I stand on Barros' back while longe-ing Ben around him.

ing the horse with the whip will be the signal for immobility as well as the "off" button for other exercises.

2 Lead your horse into the rectangle, bring him to a halt, and let him stand there while you stand outside the rectangle. Stroke the horse with your whip from a distance. After a minute or two, end the exercise by leading your horse out of the rectangle, maintaining your distance. Do not forget verbal praise!

3 Working at a slightly further distance from your horse, lead him into the rectangle and halt him. Secure the end of the lead rope near the halter so the free end isn't dangling. Now use two whips, one in each hand, and stroke your horse very calmly, using long strokes on both sides of his body. Stroke him beneath his neck, on his chest, and along his forelegs; then over his back and croup to his hind legs (use a downward stroke). In this way, the horse is "encircled" and given a "touch" boundary in front and behind him. If the horse moves his head to right or the left, or drops it down, touch him lightly and gently on the head to signal him to lift it up again or straighten it out. Move from one side to the other in front of the horse and repeat the stroking on the other half of his body. Go behind the horse and back to his front. Your horse will stand quietly because he will feel comforted by the stroking and verbal praise. Reward him with treats and lead him out of the rectangle.

4 Again halt your horse in the rectangle, create an even greater distance between the two of you, and let him stand *without* being stroked. Walk around him and reward him with food if he stands quietly until the end of the exercise. If the horse wants to leave the rectangle, raise your whip in front of him as an "optical brake," and dissuade him with your voice. If your signals from a distance are not effective, calmly and in a friendly manner lead him back into the rectangle. Whenever you are not successful advancing a step, go back to the previous phase of the exercise and start again.

⑤ Finally, practice the Statue by walking around the horse without the poles as a boundary and without having the whips in your hands. Try it in other parts of the arena. If the horse has trouble moving to a new location, set the poles up in the new spot, review previous steps, and take them away later on.

If your horse does not understand a particular phase of the exercise, *connect* it with the previous one (see p. 38), or progressively reduce your demands until you find common ground.

In Brief

Starting Point: The horse at a halt.
End Goal: The horse stands motionless.
Body Language: Horse stands; trainer walks.
Voice Command: "Whoa, halt."
Whip Signal: Stroking the horse.
Repetitions: 2 to 5 times per step.
Equipment: Halter, lead rope, two dressage whips.
Training Area: Arena or fenced-in area.
Preparation: Lowering the horse's head.
To End the Exercise: Drive the horse forward.

Backing-Up

I have determined that it is helpful to practice Backing-Up before you begin training your horse tricks, particularly before teaching the Spanish Walk. Horses can be asked to move backward at a very young age, and stepping backward is a simple but effective suppling exercise. Although horses basically do not like Backing-Up, if you proceed step-by-step in a positive atmosphere, this distaste for the exercise soon evaporates. With a great deal of practice and many treats, your horse will Back Up on command, anytime, anywhere.

I use different variations and leading positions for Backing-Up: Depending on the horse's ability to turn, and the degree of turning required, I place myself in front of him, close beside him, or behind him to one side. It is best to begin this exercise along the arena fence or wall, and you should be sure to practice each step on both sides of the horse.

In Brief

Starting Point: Halt.
End Goal: The horse moves backward on cue, even around obstacles, with the trainer positioned behind him.
Body Language: The exercise involves the following scenarios:
a) The trainer turned toward the horse's tail and moving forward in the direction she is looking.
b) The trainer looking in the same direction as the horse and, like the horse, moving backward.
c) The trainer behind and to one side of the horse as both move backward.
Voice Command: "Back," or another command of your choice.
Repetitions: Two to five times each step, depending on the horse.
Equipment: Halter, lead rope, two longe lines, a longeing surcingle (optional), two whips (one with a long lash).
Training Area: Arena or fenced-in area.
Preparation: N/A
To End the Exercise: Energetically drive the horse forward.

Before you begin, I would like to remind you to acknowledge every little success with a pause, verbal praise, food rewards, and stroking.

1 Begin alongside the arena fence or wall. Stand at the horse's head, looking toward his tail, and hold him close to the halter with your right hand. Shorten the lead by making two loops in the rope. Hold the whip in your left hand, and at the beginning of the exercise, "wave" the whip up-and-down in front of the horse's nose several times. Give the command "Back," and touch the horse on the outside of his left shoulder with the whip, while at the same time tugging gently on the lead. Express your desire for him to back with your body language—stand upright and "make yourself large." If your horse does not react by moving backward, walk toward him. The horse should react to this movement by stepping backward. Practice this step on both sides of the horse.

2 Repeat the first step of this exercise for several days, until your horse willingly steps backward without being touched with the whip or having his halter tugged. If he does not progress, you may have to "speak" more clearly with the whip. It should just be uncomfortable enough for the horse that in the future, he anticipates the touching and moves backward of his own volition.

Next, as your horse moves backward, turn around so you face the same way he does (rather than toward his tail). As you turn, renew

the command to back up so that he continues despite your different position. The command should always consist of voice, body language, and movement of the whip. After several steps backward, reward him effusively, and after a moment's pause, repeat the exercise.

③ When your horse is working well at Step 2 of the exercise, move on: Begin facing the same direction as the horse, cue him to back, and then walk backward alongside him. Remember, as you increase the difficulty of the exercise, it may be necessary to periodically go back to using your voice, and touching or waving the whip in front of the horse, to complete the step successfully.

④ Now train the horse to Back Up even when there is distance between you. Face the same direction as the horse, but this time with about 5 feet between you, and encourage him to Back Up with your voice, the signal on the lead rope, and a back-and-forth movement of the whip. Walk backward along with him. After several good, clean steps, halt the horse and reward him.

⑤ Begin as you did in Step 4; however, this time, it is helpful to use a longe line to allow you to work with your horse from a greater distance. As you Back Up, move backward more quickly than the horse so that when you halt him, you are standing 5 feet away from the horse, but at his croup, rather than his head.

⑥ In this step you need a whip with a long lash. Begin in the position in which you ended in Step 5 (at the horse's croup, facing front), give the verbal command to Back Up, and use your body language and the whip to signal the horse to move backward. Again, Back Up more quickly than the horse so that when you halt, you are actually behind the horse, although still to the side of him. If your horse does not step backward, stretch the whip out in front of him and strike the whip lash one or more times against the ground or the arena fence. (For added challenge, you can now try this step with the longe line secured to a surcingle or saddle—as in the pictures below—and only your voice, whips, and body position to cue your horse. This demonstrates how important it is for the halt on voice command to be confirmed—see p. 32.)

⑦ Start where you ended in Step 6, behind your horse, and from that position ask him to move backward. Ask for a halt after several good steps.

⑧ Repeat Step 7, only this time try it in the middle of the arena (or away from the fence line or wall). Your horse should now willingly, without tension, and in an engaged, step backward with you.

⑨ Ask your horse to yield the hindquarters to the left or the right while he is Backing-Up. Return to the sides of the arena so you have a fence or wall for a boundary and do a few

normal turns on the forehand. Then, take your place behind the horse and direct the hindquarters toward the inside by touching them on the outside with the whip. The horse should turn the hindquarters inward as he steps backward. Repeat this in the other direction.

10 Move the exercise to the middle of the arena. You can make this step easier for your horse to learn by using a longeing surcingle and a second longe line, so there is one line on each side of the horse, thus framing the hindquarters (as in ground-driving). Your horse will likely yield to the touch of the longe lines as he does to the touch of the whip. With the support of these "touching aids" on either side of him, he will quickly comprehend that he should follow you backward, and move in the same direction as you. Once he understands this, hold the longe lines away from his body and use only your voice and whip. Your horse should now follow you backward without the lines to guide him.

11 Now, teach your horse to back in a slalom pattern: While Backing-Up, touch him with one longe line on the side of the hindquarters that you want him to yield, let him take a step or two, then touch him with the other longe line on the opposite side of the hindquarters, so that he yields them in the other direction. Once he understands this step, try it without touching him with the longe lines, but only with the whip, and only when necessary.

12 Place five cones, poles, or tires in a straight line and back your horse through them. Start in the position used in Step 1—next to the horse's head, facing his tail. Then, in gradually stages as before, work your way to a position behind him and some distance away.

13 As you and your horse gain confidence, you can increase the difficulty of this exercise by performing it in various tight spots—through a Ribbon Wall (see p. 70) or around barrels, for example. Always walk your horse forward through a new obstacle, first. Then, position yourself near his head while he maneuvers through it backward. Only once it goes well with you near his head for reassurance should you gradually work your way back to the ideal position behind your horse.

14 Raise the degree of difficulty once again by maneuvering through an "L" or a labyrinth of poles. First, lead your horse forward through "L," halt him, and then back him it with you at his head. Gradually move to your position behind him.

15 Weeks have likely passed since the first steps of this lesson. You probably feel as if you have praised your horse constantly, and no doubt you have found yourself exiting the arena with a big smile on your face more often than not. You have already learned a lot about what works when teaching your horse a specific movement—and your horse has learned to pay attention to a variety of cues and to tune in

to your body language. You have fumbled, organized, and analyzed—and have been patient in your interactions with your horse. Now it is time to experience the first dose of satisfaction. Congratulations!

Your first two tricks are in the bag, and you can begin showing them off. Once you can move your horse backward on cue, through all sorts of obstacles, and on straight or curved lines, prepare a little demonstration of his backing skills. The audience—family, friends, barn-mates—will be mighty impressed, and your eyes will sparkle with pride because only you know the effort that underlies the act.

Stepping Sideways

1. Lead your horse to the middle of the arena. You should be positioned on his left side. Ask him to yield his forehand to you for a few steps, with his hind legs crossing. Then change sides and repeat.

2. Attach the lead rope to the right side of the halter, and stand at the front of the horse so you can reach around and touch him on his left side with the whip. You want him to yield to the whip, Stepping Sideways.

3. Now stand on the horse's right side with your left hand holding the horse at the halter. With your right arm reach under his neck and touch the horse on the left side of his belly with the whip so he moves his hindquarters toward you, to the right. When your horse understands this, praise him profusely.

If Step 3 does not work, repeat Step 2, and do not be shy about "clearly" touching your horse with the whip, if necessary. When he manages Step 2 successfully return to Step 3. (This way, you "connect" a known exercise with a new one—see p. 38.)

④ Now practice yielding to the right from the same position, but this time reach your arm over the horse's back. Touch the horse on his left hip. Because of the preceding steps, your horse should understand the cue and yield toward you. It goes without saying that for symmetry's sake, you should practice this exercise on both sides.

⑤ Once the horse has the hang of it, remove his halter and repeat the previous steps with him at liberty.

⑥ If necessary, grab onto your horse's mane and use it to control him or help guide him, as you would do with a halter and lead.

⑦ Ask your horse to move toward you from a greater distance. Control his head position by holding your left hand out toward it. If the horse rushes forward when you cue him with the whip, position a second whip in front of him and vibrate it up and down near his head, or touch his chest with it. You can also move to one side of the arena and ask the horse to move along it toward you, using the fence or wall to prevent forward movement. Continue to increase the distance between you and the horse.

And What Does This Trick Have to Do with Riding?

When training most tricks we cannot, thank goodness, employ force and expect to see results. If you use too much pressure in early steps of the exercises, the horse will simply avoid the tricks when you try to work him at liberty.

Unfortunately, when you are on a horse's back it is possible to clamp the horse into a "vice" comprised of whip, spurs, and reins. It is often the case that horses are therefore forced to perform by the infliction of excruciating pain and/or stress. This is to the detriment of willing harmonious cooperation between horse and rider, and has no place in real horse training.

In Brief

Starting Point: Halt.
End Goal: The horse moves sideways toward the trainer, at liberty.
Body Language: The trainer's body should be at a 90-degree angle to the horse.
Voice Command: "Side (ways)," or the command of your choice.
Repetitions: Two or more times each step, depending on the horse.
Equipment: Halter, lead rope, whip.
Training Area: Arena or fenced-in area.
Preparation: Yielding the forehand toward the trainer in-hand.
To End the Exercise: Drive the horse forward or touch his side opposite the direction in which he is moving with the whip.

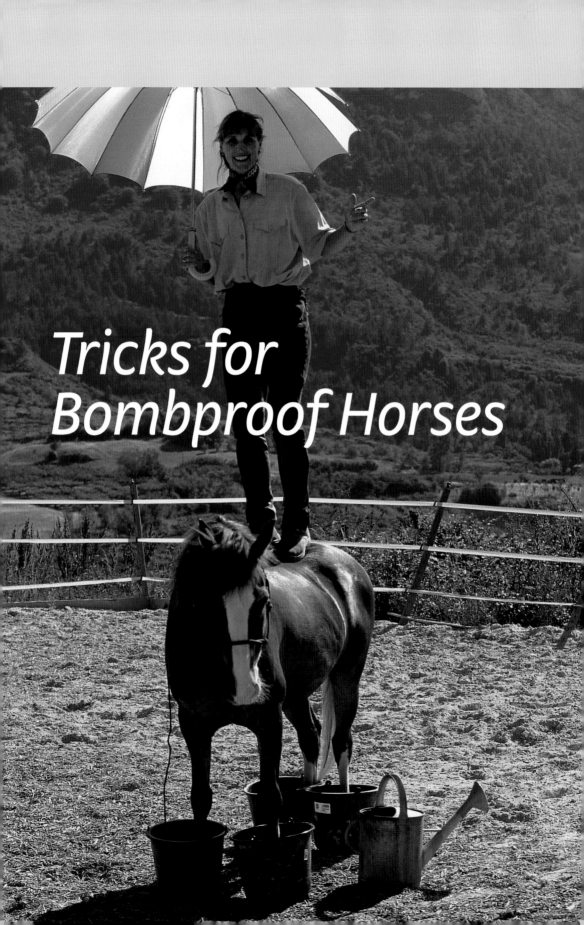

Tricks for Bombproof Horses

Riding without a Bridle

Riding without a bridle is great fun for the horse, as well as the rider. The horse's expression changes so much—from movements performed with a bridle to those performed without one—that observers almost get more out of the experience then you do! Have someone record you riding your horse without a bridle, and see for yourself how beautifully, freely, and with what radiant expression your horse moves.

① Ride your horse in an enclosed arena with his bridle on and a neck ring (I recommend Linda Tellington-Jones' Liberty Neck Ring—see p. xiii for information) around his neck so that as you introduce the neck ring's pressure, you can still use the bridle if your horse is not obedient. Knot your reins with enough length so they do not influence your horse's mouth, and let them lie on his neck. The neck ring should be large enough so that you can hold it in your hands without leaning forward.

Lay your fingers over the neck ring from above, with your thumbs pointing toward each other. This way you can easily raise and lower the neck ring. The neck ring is not to be in constant contact with the horse's neck but only employed to give a signal. For the time being, ride only at a walk.

② *Halting* All signals with the neck ring should be given in a pulsing manner—in other words, a give-and-take on the ring rather than a steady pull. To halt, position the ring low at the base of the neck near the horse's chest and say "Whoa, halt." Your horse should already know the meaning of the voice command combined with the touch on his chest. If your horse does not halt, lift the neck ring so that it is positioned right under his throat and tug-and-release until your horse understands what you want and responds correctly. If necessary, further reinforce this signal with one that the horse knows—namely, touching him on the chest with your whip or crop. Halt your horse after a few steps and praise him generously with food when he stops. Repeat this many times.

It is really vitally important that your horse can absolutely be relied upon to halt

on command. So, with this lesson especially, let him profit from the experience by giving him treats. He will get the idea that it really pays off to stop, and so his reliability will increase.

Turning To turn *right*, move your *left* shoulder slightly forward and lay the neck ring on the *left* side of the horse's neck. You are essentially "neck-reining" as you do when riding in a Western saddle and bridle. To turn *left*, reverse your aids: Bring your *right* shoulder forward and touch the horse on the *right* side of his neck. (Note: In the photo, I am demonstrating turning on Tabea without a bridle—but at this point, you should still have a bridle on for safety.)

Accompany the movement with appropriate leg and weight aids: Displace your weight in the direction you want to turn. When turning left, your left leg is at the girth, without adding pressure. Your right (outside) leg is slightly behind the girth. It may be necessary to use the outside leg quite strongly if your horse is slow to respond to the neck ring to make a turn.

Use your legs to make it clear to the horse that on the right, "the door is closed," but on the left, it is "open." In addition, because your horse knows from your earlier groundwork that a vibration of the whip is a signal to yield away, you can use the whip in a waving motion at his head level on the outside, or touch his outside shoulder with it. If he still has difficulty turning in the neck ring, take a step or two back in training and revisit something he is comfortable with.

4. When you know that your "brakes" work well you can begin to trot. At first trot only a few steps so it is easy to reduce your horse's pace. The worst case is the "brakes" do not work and your horse's speed increases in a completely uncontrolled way. Should this happen, use your reins to bring your horse to a complete halt, and start again.

5. When you have practiced trotting and halting, and if you feel comfortable on your horse at the canter, go ahead and let your horse canter while you steer with the neck ring. At first, bring him back to the trot, walk, and halt after only a few canter strides. Reward the well-behaved horse with praise and treats.

6. Practice circles and serpentines at the walk and trot.

7. When you have thoroughly practiced the previous steps and feel secure enough, remove the horse's bridle and ride with the neck ring alone. Start with the walk, trot, and halt.

8. Finally, let your horse canter with his head "free" and only use the neck ring to guide him—you'll be amazed at how exhilarating both you and your horse will find it!

Statue with "Racket Sack"

It is always a very good idea to prepare your horse for situations that could make him spook. This exercise not only exposes your horse to new stimuli, it also allows you to determine how relaxed and "bombproof" he already is. I've taken the now common concept of "sacking out" and given it my own spin: The lessons that follow are meant to prepare your horse for all kinds of situations, and make him safer and more competent in everything he does, as well as add a few more tricks to your repertoire. I'll begin with the Racket Sack—essentially, a noisemaker (a bag filled with cans, stones, and other "rattley" objects).

1 Begin by asking your horse to stand still in a box made of ground poles, as you did in the first Statue exercise (see p. 47). Fill an empty soda can with several stones so that when you shake it, you can hear quite a bit of noise. First stand in front of the horse and show him the can (hold the lead rope until you know how he is going to react). Slowly begin to shake it. If your horse remains quiet and still, secure the lead rope, give him the command to remain still, and circle him once, calmly, rattling the can as you go.

2 Take an empty burlap or cloth sack and touch the horse all over his body with it. (*Note:* I start with a burlap bag and move on later to a plastic bag, which is noisier and thus more frightening to some horses.) The horse should let himself be rubbed everywhere on his body. If he is uncomfortable with this step, practice rubbing him with it every day when he is on the cross-ties or secured in his stall for grooming or tacking-up.

3 Now take the sack and shake it to make some noise. Begin at the horse's head, then circle him while shaking the sack.

4 Put the soda can you used in Step 1 into the sack. Circle the horse while shaking that.

5 Fill several more cans with small stones, put them in the sack, and now create a *lot* of noise, repeating the circling and shaking.

6 When your horse has demonstrated obedience and quietness, up the ante by filling a plastic sack with your cans and stones (it is now a true Racket Sack). Shake it under his belly and throw it over his back. (Note: Prac-

tice a toss over his back with the empty bag, first, and then maybe throw the full bag over a fence, so that you get a feel for the degree of momentum you need in your throw. If you throw the Racket Sack over the horse with too little momentum, and it lands on his back, you'll give him a real shock!)

7 Finally, drop the Racket Sack to the ground with a "crash" and then drag it behind you as you walk around the horse.

The less comfortable your horse is with a step, the more time you should allow for him to learn it. Break down the individual steps over several days.

In Brief

Starting Point: Halt in the square of poles.
End Goal: The horse performs the Statue even while a noisy sack is thrown over his back and dragged around him.
Body Language: Maintain a calm and confident stance as you move around the horse's body.
Voice Command: "Whoa, halt," "Stand," or a command of your choice.
Repetitions: Two to three times each step, depending on the horse.
Equipment: Halter, lead rope, four ground poles, six soda cans filled with small stones, a strong burlap sack, a plastic sack, a cord or rope with which to tie the racket sack and drag it.
Training Area: Arena or fenced-in area.
Preparation: Practice halting and waiting patiently.
To End the Exercise: Allow the horse to move forward out of the box.

In Motion with "Racket Sack"

When Statue with Racket Sack has been mastered, I suggest that you and your horse move around the arena, dragging the noisy sack along behind you. I like to intersperse regular workouts with this exercise—or example, when I longe my mare Tabea I might interrupt the longe lesson, get the Racket Sack, and practice the following:

1 Begin with a longe line attached to a halter or cavesson. Allow your horse to sniff the Racket Sack. Lead the horse with the longe line, allowing about 6 feet between you, and drag the Racket Sack along the ground in that space between you and your horse. If you did the prior exercise correctly, you will find that your horse is not the least bit anxious but instead

follows the sack curiously. Go back-and-forth diagonally across the arena, and every so often come to a halt. When your horse has mastered this, secure the longe line to the horse's surcingle or saddle (so you are no longer leading the horse with it, but it is there if you need it).

2 Trot alongside your horse, dragging the Racket Sack behind you. Watch how your horse responds to this. Do the louder noises frighten him? Or does he calmly follow beside or behind you? If the horse is anxious or insecure, stop immediately and let him think about the situation before asking him to trot just a few steps once again. Slowly accustom him to the new situation.

3 For those horses that are very bomb-proof and comfortable with this exercise, you can attempt the following challenge (I do this with Ben, who can walk backward at liberty and is calm with the Racket Sack): I place the sack on the ground underneath Ben's belly and pull the rope attached to the sack between his hind legs. I then give Ben the signal to Back Up (see p. 50). He walks backward as I walk backward, and I keep tension on the rope so the sack stays between Ben's hind legs. This exercise has a very high degree of difficulty. For young, spooky Tabea, it is still unthinkable.

In Brief

Starting Point: Statue with Racket Sack (see p. 58).
End Goal: The Racket Sack can be dragged between the horse's hind legs as the horse moves backward, at liberty, on cue.
Body Language: Changes over the course of the exercise:
a) To slow the horse, move to a position beside and a little in front of him.
b) To drive the horse on, move to a position beside and a little behind him.
Voice Command: Includes your commands "Whoa, halt," or "Stand," as well as "Walk," "Trot," and "Back," or other commands of your choice.
Repetitions: Two to five times each step, depending on the horse.
Equipment: Halter or cavesson, longe line, six soda cans filled with small stones, a burlap or plastic bag, a cord or rope to tie and drag it with.
Training Area: Arena or fenced-in area.
Preparation: The ability to walk and trot in-hand in a controlled way, as well as a prompt, obedient halt, and a willing Back-Up.
To End the Exercise: Halt and put aside the Racket Sack.

Statue with Umbrella

Here's another variation of the Statue combined with sacking-out techniques: Circle the horse with items even larger than the Racket Sack—for example, with a large golf umbrella or a bunch of balloons. Training with an umbrella is a lot of fun, as well as teaching your horse to react safely and quietly to all possible visual stimuli—a necessity both in the "trick world," and in the "real world."

1 Begin with the horse in Statue, show him the umbrella—closed, at first, and I also advise using a small, dark, plain one before later moving to a large colorful version—and walk around him carrying it.

2 Next, touch the horse everywhere on his body with the closed umbrella so that he learns that this object, too, is totally harmless.

3 Slowly, and in fractions, open the umbrella in front of the horse. Open it a little more, and let him get used to it, then a little more, and so on. Constantly enlarge its appearance until you can open it all the way.

4 The next step is to hold the umbrella above the horse's back and move it around—up toward his neck and head. This is very frightening for some horses because objects and movement above and behind mean "danger." Lift the umbrella over the horse for only a moment and then bring it to one side again. Lengthen these moments until you can hold the open umbrella over the horse's head for as long as you please and the horse remains calm.

5 Ask your horse to walk forward as you walk alongside him, holding the umbrella over his (as though it is raining).

6 Stand your horse next to a mounting block and ask him to remain still as you walk around him with the open umbrella, and clamber up and down off the mounting block, holding the umbrella over him.

7 Climb up on the mounting block with the closed umbrella and open it over the horse's back. When you can do that safely, go one step further and get on your horse, first with the closed umbrella, and then open the umbrella as you are sitting in the saddle. (*Note:* You may need an assistant to hold your horse the first time you try this exercise. I also recommend wearing a helmet.)

In Brief

Starting Point: The Statue (see p. 47).
End Goal: Trainer stands on the horse's croup while holding an opened umbrella.
Body Language: Move around the horse in a calm, confident manner.
Voice Command: "Whoa, halt," "Stand," or the command of your choice.
Repetitions: Two to three times each step, depending on the horse.
Equipment: Halter or bridle, lead rope, a small dark umbrella, a large colorful umbrella, saddle, mounting block, assistant.
Training Area: Arena or fenced-in area.
Preparation: Halting and waiting patiently, Racket Sack exercises.
To End the Exercise: Ask the horse to walk on.

8 Now try to move out of the saddle and sit behind it. Let your helper lead the horse forward a few steps. This is an important check to see if the horse is accepting of unaccustomed weight so far back. If it feels like your horse may attempt to buck (usually very, very mild, if it happens at all), halt, stroke your horse, and

talk to him quietly until you ask him to walk on again. You can also end the session at that point and try again the following day. Move progressively further back, until you have gained the horse's total acceptance and can sit on his croup.

9 If you are brave and your horse is quiet, try mounting him bareback with umbrella in hand, and bit by bit moving back to his croup as before.

10 When you have practiced Step 9 for several days with your horse willingly participating, move from sitting to a kneeling position, and from there to standing up. The more time you give this exercise, the more secure your horse will become (and the more balanced your own position will be).

11 Now combine all the individual steps in this exercise into one trick performance. Repeat the steps on the ground, close the umbrella, mount up, open the umbrella, close it

again, scoot backward to the croup, first kneel and then lift yourself into a standing position holding the still closed umbrella. Move the umbrella back and forth in front of you over your horse's back, then very slowly open it. Ta da! End the exercise with the reverse step-by-step process: close umbrella, kneel, sit, dismount—huge rewards for the horse!

Statue with Buckets

While working with my Anglo-Arab mare, Monodie, I developed a variation of the Statue trick involving buckets. Monodie would put each foot into a separate bucket while I jumped on her back, stood on her croup, opened an umbrella, and finally, had an assistant pour water into the buckets.

Plan to spend a great deal of time on this "combo trick" because each element must be perfected individually.

1 As always, begin with the Statue and show the horse the various objects you'll be using. Review the Statue with Umbrella exercise (see p. 62). The first step of this exercise is to place one of your horse's feet in a bucket. So

put a bucket on the ground and let the horse nuzzle it. Touch the horse's forelegs, body, and belly with the bucket so that he realizes the bucket's touch is nothing to fear. Now ask your horse to lift one front leg, take it in your hand, and put it down in front of the bucket. Reward him. Repeat, but this time put the leg *into* the bucket. Praise your horse lavishly.

2 Take the same bucket and ask the horse to put his other front hoof in it. Then work on his hind feet. Ask the horse to put each hoof into a bucket individually before bringing a second bucket into the picture. When he is comfortable with you moving around him, placing each foot in the bucket, leave one foot in the bucket and introduce another. Repeat Step 1. Add a third and fourth bucket.

3 With the horse standing in all four buckets, mount and gradually assume the standing position on his croup, as explained on p. 63. (Note: You may need an assistant at his head the first few times you try this step.)

4 Now teach the horse to let you sprinkle his legs with water. Your horse is probably familiar with a hose and spray nozzle. Transitioning to the trickle from a watering can

In Brief

Starting Point: The Statue (see p. 47).
End Goal: Horse with all four legs in buckets and trainer standing on his croup with an open umbrella.
Body Language: Move calmly and confidently around the horse as he remains still.
Voice Command: "Whoa, halt," "Stand," or a command of your choice.
Repetitions: Two or three times each step, depending on the horse
Equipment: Halter, four sturdy buckets, watering can, large colorful umbrella.
Training Area: Arena or fenced-in area.
Preparation: Halting and patiently waiting; Racket Sack exercises, and Statue with Umbrella (p. 63).
To End the Exercise: Ask the horse to walk on.

shouldn't be difficult. Start by bringing a full watering can with you to the riding arena, and let your horse watch as you water the ground around him. Then sprinkle one foreleg, then the other, and eventually, the hind legs. Ask him to stand in all four buckets and sprinkle his legs again.

5 Now put the steps together. Ask your horse to stand in buckets, mount him with a large colorful umbrella in hand, stand up on his croup, open the umbrella, and ask your assistant to sprinkle his legs. Vary the individual elements, combining two of them, then three, then four.

Statue with Sheet

One last variation on the Statue that I recommend is "wrapping" your horse in a large sheet—first fabric and then plastic. This exercise requires a lot of effort, but when completed successfully, your horse will be better able to deal with large visual distractions, flapping and dragging sensations on and around his body, and the sounds that are associated with them.

It is of the utmost importance to proceed slowly with this exercise, with attention to the details. Plan to practice it over the course of many days so that the exercise does not become dangerous due to rushing or impatience on your part. Do not attempt this trick with easily excitable, explosive horses; only try it if your horse has already proven his reliability to you many times, and only if he has mastered all the exercises I have explained in the Tricks for Bombproof Horses section up to now.

1 Begin this exercise working with a bed sheet folded in half. (After going through the steps with a bed sheet, if you want to, you can repeat them with a small, and then large, sheet of plastic.) Show your horse the sheet, shake it, wave it, flap it so it makes noise. Circle the horse while doing this—he should remain standing in the Statue. Then touch his body with the folded sheet and lay it across his back.

2 Now unfold the bed sheet so it is full size (or if you are working with plastic, get the larger sheet of plastic) and repeat Step 1. The sheet should be large enough so that you can completely cover your horse with it. Lay the sheet across his back.

3 Now "wrap" your horse in the sheet—pull it down over his hindquarters and up over his withers. For safety's sake, I recommend holding the lead rope while you do this. Also, always keep a corner of the sheet in your hand. This way, if your horse spooks and runs off, you can immediately pull the sheet off so he does not panic when he realizes he is covered in a sheet and alone.

In Brief

Starting Point: The Statue (see p. 47).
End Goal: The horse is covered in a plastic sheet.
Body Language: Move calmly and confidently around the horse.
Voice Command: "Whoa, halt," "Stand," or other command of your choice.
Repetitions: Two to three times each step, depending on the horse.
Equipment: Halter, lead rope, twin-size flat bed sheet, plastic sheet 3 by 3 feet, plastic sheet 6½ by 6½ feet.
Training Area: Arena or fenced-in area.
Preparation: Halting and waiting patiently, previous Statue exercises.
To End the Exercise: Ask the horse to walk on.

4 Finally, for the really bombproof individuals, you can cut holes for the ears and pull the sheet up over the horse's neck and down over his head. This demands immense amounts of trust on the part of the horse. Do not attempt it unless you are quite sure of your horse's confidence and mastery of the preceding exercises—including the Racket Sack exercises. If necessary, revisit the Racket Sack from time to time to ensure your horse remains calm in exciting situations. Some tricks I can "leave in the drawer" for months on end and still expect them to be performed on a moment's notice, but the ones in this chapter need consistent work and should be "worked up to" when they haven't been attempted for a period of time.

Tricks for
Brave Horses

The "Ribbon Wall"

The "Ribbon Wall" is an excellent way to prepare a horse for walking or jumping through a sheet of paper, a banner, or a ring, should a dramatic entry be called for during a presentation or horse show.

1 First you must construct a "curtain" of ribbons or streamers. I like to use surveyor's tape, which you can find reasonably priced at a building supply/home improvement center. Cut 30 strips, about 6 1/2 feet long each. You also need three strong, flat pieces of wood for your frame—two that are about 8 feet long (the upright supports) and one about 6 1/2 feet (the crossbar). Note: The wider you build your frame (the longer the crossbar) the easier the exercise will be for your horse. Fasten the wood pieces together into a "U" shape, secure the ribbon strips onto the crossbar, and then erect your Ribbon Wall between two stable jump standards (bind the uprights to the standards with rope or duct tape). Warning: Do not train this trick outdoors in windy conditions because your Ribbon Wall could fall over. Even in an indoor arena you must be sure the prop is sturdy. It helps to build it next to the arena fence or wall.

2 Separate the ribbons in the center and tie half to each side, thus creating an opening in the middle. A basic rule when training this trick against the fence or wall: Always walk on the inside (toward the middle of the ring) so if your horse moves quickly, you have an "escape route." This means when you walk through the Ribbon Wall to the right, you are on your horse's right side, and vice versa.

3 Lead your horse to the Ribbon Wall, halt, and ask him to lower his head (see p. 42). Watch how your horse behaves around this new obstacle. If he is nervous, stroke him with the whip and let him sniff both sides of the Ribbon Wall. Let the horse observe the situation, evaluate it, and finally, accept it (see p. 14).

4 Walk briskly through the middle of the "wall" with your horse. On your next pass, halt with your horse in the "doorway" and stroke him with the whip as you praise him. If the horse fidgets and refuses to stand still, walk on and try again.

In Brief

Starting Point: Horse walks up to a curtain of streamers—the "Ribbon Wall."
End Goal: Horse jumps over an obstacle and through the Ribbon Wall.
Body Language: Vary your leading positions, on both sides of the horse, as appropriate.
Voice Command: "Walk on," "Tr-ot," "Whoa, halt," and/or the commands of your choice.
Repetitions: Two or three times, depending on the horse.
Equipment: Halter, lead rope, about 200 feet of surveyor's tape, three strong thin slats of wood, two jump standards, a large piece of plastic or tarp about 2 feet by 6½ feet, several large paper sheets about 13 feet by 13 feet, raised cavalletti.
Training Area: Preferably an indoor arena.
Preparation: Controlled pace in all gaits, halt on command, the ability to free-jump over cavalletti.
To End the Exercise: Ask your horse for the Statue (see p. 47).

5 Ask the horse to stand in front of the Ribbon Wall, lengthen the lead rope, and walk through the obstacle first. (Your horse should wait in Statue until you give the signal for him to follow.) Give your horse the voice command to walk on, and wait for him to join you on the other side. Repeat the process, this time letting a few ribbons hang down in the middle.

6 Increase the degree of difficulty every day. Continually let additional ribbons down so that the "doorway" in the middle gets progres-

sively smaller until it disappears altogether. If at any point your horse becomes frightened by the plastic ribbons, stop the exercise on the spot. Revisit the "sacking-out" we did in Statue with "Racket Sack" and Statue with Sheet (see pp. 58 and 68). Touch your horse all over with towels, plastic bags, and then extra pieces of ribbon like those that hang from the Ribbon Wall. Finally, stand your horse in front of the Ribbon Wall and "connect" the details—stroke him with a ribbon and then walk him through the obstacle.

7 Ask your horse to walk backward through the Ribbon Wall. First, do so at his head,

using the halter and lead rope, then move on to backing at liberty as we practiced earlier in the book (see p. 50). Walk forward partway through the Ribbon Wall and then immediately reverse, going slowly backward through it. Repeat this, each time going further through the "wall" before asking the horse to Back Up. When your horse can complete this step, it confirms that he understands the lesson 100 percent and does not fear the obstacle at all.

8 When you are ready for an extra challenge, take a sheet of heavy plastic or tarp and cut it into four pieces 20 inches wide and about 6¹/₂ feet long. Fasten these to your crossbar in place of the ribbons. Begin again with Step 1 of the exercise. When your horse goes through these heavier, wider "ribbons," tape the set on the left and the set on the right together with duct tape so there is only one gap in the center for the horse to go through, and far more resistance.

9 Now, believe it or not, your horse is ready to "burst" through a solid paper "wall"! The most difficult aspect is building a very secure obstacle. (You will probably need more time to build the paper "wall" than you will need for getting your horse to go through it!) In any case, be sure to test the stability of your construction before attempting this step of the trick. Secure a 13- by 13-foot sheet of paper between your jump standards. Perforate the middle (you can make a line of smallish holes with a pair of scissors) so the wall tears very easily upon contact. Start again with Step 1 of this exercise and teach your horse to walk through the new obstacle.

10 Now construct a jump with cavalletti (this should be at a height the horse takes seriously) on the long side of the arena, a few strides away from the Ribbon Wall. (Note: Begin this step by returning to the Ribbon Wall

with the sides tied back and an opening in the middle.) Have your horse jump the cavalletti and then go through the Ribbon Wall. Gradually let the ribbons down and repeat. Then, combine both elements: Set up the "open" Ribbon Wall (with the sides fastened back) close enough to the cavalletti that the horse jumps "through" the "wall." Gradually let the ribbons down. If your horse is confident and you can build a very secure obstacle, you can advance to the wider pieces of plastic, and even the "solid" sheet of paper.

Standing on Pallets or a Pedestal

This series of exercises includes Atop the Mountain (see Step 4), which I mentioned earlier as a good suppling exercise because the horse's hind feet must be brought close to his front feet in order for him to stand on a small surface. If you want to use this trick in a performance, you can build a special pedestal of a size, shape, and color to suit your needs. Construct one at a reasonable height and width. You don't want your horse to injure himself with a sudden jump off a too-high pedestal, or because a slight movement widens his stance and causes him to straddle a too-narrow surface.

1 Lay six pallets together in a square. (I've covered mine with colorful non-skid fabric in the photos.) Allow your horse to look at them, nuzzle them, and then lead him up onto their surface and across to the other side. (Note: If your horse is wary of stepping onto the pallets, tempt him with treats.) Halt and praise the horse. Turn to cross again, but this time, halt him before he steps onto the pallets, again when he is on them, and once more right after he steps off the other side. During the halts, stroke the horse's legs with your whip

In Brief

Starting Point: Horse approaches and stands on wooden pallets lying beside one another.
End Goal: Horse stands on stacked pallets or a raised pedestal.
Body Language: Stand on the pallets and pedestal, as well, and use driving signals to urge the horse on.
Voice Command: "Step up," "And up!" or the command of your choice.
Repetitions: Six or more times each step, depending on the horse.
Equipment: Halter, lead rope, nine sturdy wooden pallets. (Make sure the surface is solid or the slats are so close together there is no chance of the horse's foot being caught. In addition, "soften" the corners with a hammer or duct tape.)
Training Area: Arena or fenced-in area.
Preparation: Practice walking over plastic tarps, boards, and pieces of carpeting.
To End the Exercise: Drive the horse forward or away from you.

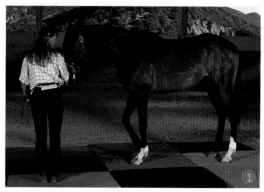

(see p. 47) and praise him with a quiet voice. Now, cross again, halt on top of the pallets, and back your horse several steps. Rearrange the pallet configuration so they are laid out in a long line (like a bridge) rather than a square (like a dance floor) and repeat Step 1.

② Now, with four pallets laid out in a "bridge," stack four more on top of them so your horse has to step up higher. Repeat Step 1. Note: If your horse does not want to climb onto the stacked pallets, place a single pallet in line with the double pallets, so his "step ups" are less exaggerated. Once your horse has mastered the row of double-stacked pallets, increase the difficulty by stacking a row of three, three pallets high (nine pallets total). Repeat Step 1.

③ Now decrease the number of pallets to one (we're creating a "pedestal")—the exercise becomes more difficult because the surface area is smaller. In order to "contain" the horse on the small surface, we must get him to "think backward" and always be ready to stop immediately, on cue. Before approaching the pedestal, walk the horse forward, halt him, and immediately as him to Back Up. Repeat this several times. Follow this preparatory exercise by leading your horse to the pedestal and let him put his *forefeet only* on its surface—then immediately ask him to back off it. Praise him. (Don't forget!) Repeat several times. Finally,

allow your horse to step all the way onto the pedestal (he'll want to, by now), and you'll find that the result of getting your horse to "think backward" is an obedient halt on the pedestal's limited surface. Back him off (backing off is easier on his loins) and try again, from a different side of the pedestal.

④ Stack two pallets, creating a higher pedestal. Repeat Step 3. When it is time for your horse to climb all the way onto the pedestal, direct each of his legs individually, proceeding slowly and quietly so your horse can find the correct balance. Once he is on the stacked pallets, halt him, praise him, and back him off, just as slowly and leg-by-leg, as when climbing up. Repeat from every side of the pedestal. Then add a third pallet to increase the height once again. This is what I call "Atop the Moutain"!

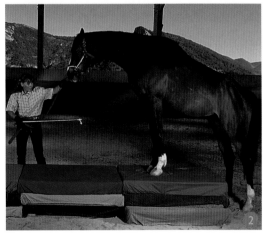

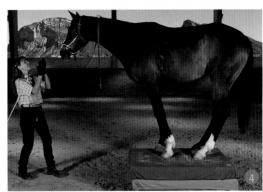

5 For performance purposes, you can create many variations of this trick. You can have your horse stand on the pedestal with his front feet while asking him to yield his haunches around it. (Note: I don't believe the opposite scenario is acceptable—hind feet on the pedestal while the forefeet yield around—because of the strain it puts on the horse's body.) I also build multi-level pedestals and work with several of my horses at the same time, to increase the entertainment value!

The Balance Beam

Note: This exercise is not appropriate for large, heavy horses.

1 First lay two narrow but very sturdy boards (2 inches thick and 10 inches wide is best—they should be 8 to 10 feet long) next to each other on the ground, and then two more behind those so that there is a relatively long, and reasonably wide surface to start on. Lead your horse up to the boards and allow him to look at them and nuzzle them. Begin at your horse's head and lead him up onto the boards and all the way down their length, and off the other end. Repeat, this time halting before he climbs on, somewhere in the middle, and after he climbs off. Try again, now lengthening the lead rope and cueing him from a distance. (When you are really confident, you can try Step 1 at liberty, as I am doing with Ben in the photo.)

2 Remove one row of boards so the width of the wooden "path" is cut in half. Repeat Step 1, making it clear to your horse that he should stay on the surface of the board. Every step must be made slowly and deliberately. If your horse has trouble keeping his feet on the board, lay ground poles along either side to give him a visual guide. Work close to the horse's head and with a very short lead.

3 Now suspend the board, creating a "Balance Beam" by placing two stacked pallets under each end. (*Note:* If your board is not exceptionally thick, you may want to nail two together to strengthen the Balance Beam.) Add a row of pallets under the middle of the Balance Beam, to decrease the distance to the "ground," should the horse lose his balance and step off one side. Repeat Step 2, beginning by asking the horse to climb onto the Pedestal (the stacked pallets) before making his way across the Balance Beam (see p. 74).

4 Remove the pallets under the middle of the Balance Beam so the middle is suspended freely over the ground. Now your horse must really balance to get to the other end. Give it

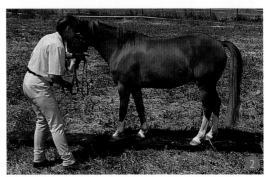

In Brief

Starting Point: Horse approaches and walks on a board laid on the ground.
End Goal: Horse walks, in balance, along a raised board ("Balance Beam").
Body Language: As when first teaching your horse to Back Up, stand at his head, facing his tail, and walk slowly backward.
Voice Command: "Up and walk on," or command of your choice.
Repetitions: Two or more times each step, depending on the horse.
Equipment: Halter, lead rope, four boards (8 to 10 feet long, 10 inches wide, 2 inches thick), nine pallets.
Training Area: Arena or fenced-in area.
Preparation: Walk your horse between an "alley" made of ground poles and over tarps or pieces of carpeting.
To End the Exercise: Drive the horse forward, away from the obstacle.

a try. This exercise requires much patience, many repetitions, and a lot of treats! Once your horse has mastered it in-hand, try it at liberty.

⑤ With an exceptionally willing and balanced horse, you can ask him to halt occasionally, or even to step backward. This is an unbelievable challenge because the horse needs an enormous degree of body awareness and trust, as well as patience, to feel his way backward on the Balance Beam. I like to reverse our positions, with Ben at liberty on the ground while I "prance" along the Balance Beam, inviting him to jump in front of me, or place his front feet upon it, as he does with the pedestal (see p. 74). Use your imagination!

The Tightrope

By now you have probably developed a taste for this type of challenge, and you are likely fascinated by your horse's improved body awareness. So let's go a step further and make a tightrope walker out of your horse!

Ben can balance his forehand on a ground pole, walking carefully along, one foot in front of the other, while his hind feet straddle the pole and tread upon the ground. I only need to be careful that he does not become too enthusiastic and too quick, because then he has to step off.

1 Drag a trench in the footing of your arena the length of a ground pole. Place a ground pole in it, and pack the footing tightly around it so it cannot roll. Allow your horse to sniff and nuzzle the pole, and step over it, familiarizing himself with the situation. Once he is comfortable with this, ask him to step over it sideways, yielding away from you, and toward you (see p. 53).

2 Ask your horse to straddle the pole lengthwise—his left feet on one side and his right feet on the other. You may be surprised how difficult this step is and how much time it takes for your horse to master it! While Ben learned this step relatively quickly, Tabea continually fell to one side or the other with her hindquarters. I can only assume she thought the pole between her feet and under her belly a very strange thing. Repeat the effort until your horse stands straddling the pole at the halt, and willingly walks forward with the pole between his legs.

3 Lay out a long, sturdy board like the one used for the Balance Beam (see p. 76). Lead your horse to one end, facing the board (perpendicular to it). Ask him to step onto it with his forefeet and step sideways (see p. 53). His forefeet should cross and stay on the board with each step (essentially side-passing with his forefeet on the board and his hind feet on the ground). This requires very calm and careful direction from you. Practice in both directions.

4 Switch back to the ground pole. Repeat Step 3. The horse now has much less "foot-room" than before, and he must aim accurately to place each forefoot precisely. Increase the number of steps you ask for each day.

5 When your horse masters Step 4, increase the difficulty of the trick again. Lead your horse to the end of the ground pole, but this time have him face it as he did when he straddled the pole in Step 2, rather than be perpendicular to it. Ask him to balance his front feet on the pole, one in front of the other. Praise him. Then ask him to walk forward with his forefeet on the pole and his hind legs straddling it. When he can do this with your help, ask him to repeat the feat at liberty. And, if he gets good enough at this, you can try the trick on a raised cavalletti!

In Brief

Starting Point: The horse steps sideways over a ground pole, in either direction.

End Goal: The horse walks his forefeet down the length of the pole while straddling it behind.

Body Language: As you did when teaching your horse to Back Up (see p. 50), position yourself at his head, facing his tail, and step back as he moves forward.

Voice Command: "Up and walk," or the command of your choice.

Repetitions: Two or more times each step, depending on the horse.

Equipment: Halter, lead rope, ground pole, a sturdy board (see p. 77).

Training Area: Arena or fenced-in area.

Preparation: Relaxation at the walk, Stepping Sideways (see p. 53) and work on the Balance Beam (see p. 76).

To End the Exercise: Energetically drive the horse forward or ask for the Statue (see p. 47).

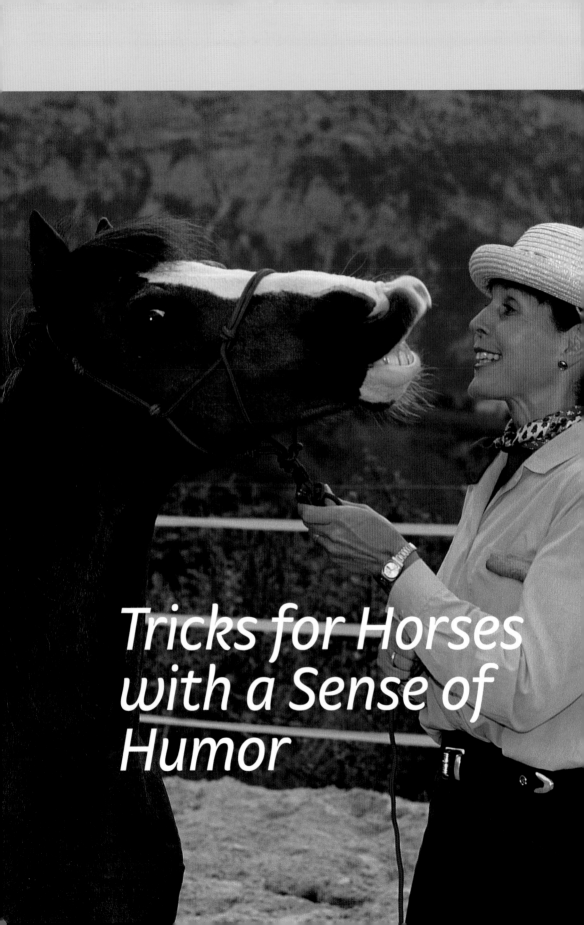

Tricks for Horses with a Sense of Humor

Crossing the Forelegs

As you become more interested in tricks and in developing a series of tricks you can perform for audiences, you will soon find that you attend shows and expos in order to "steal" other trick trainers' ideas. In fact, it was a performance of a colleague of mine—Nathalie Penquitt—where I first saw the Crossing the Forelegs trick. That was over 15 years ago!

1 In order to do this trick, your horse should have mastered the Statue (see p. 47), should allow his legs to be touched all over, and he should yield his forehand both to the left and to the right.

To begin, practice turning on the haunches—the haunches remain in place as the forehand turns around them. Stand on your horse's left, facing his tail. Hold the lead rope very close to the halter. Touch his left shoulder with the whip (or with your hand, as I am in the photos) as a signal for your horse to begin yielding his forehand away from you and turning on the haunches. It is actually the first step of a turn on the haunches that is exactly what is required for Crossing the Forelegs. So, after you have asked for a turn on the haunches several times, ask once again, but this time the instant your horse begins to move, bring the whip from the left side of the horse under the horse's neck to his right shoulder in order to quickly stop the movement. Your horse will not necessarily stop with his forelegs in the crossed over position—it is more likely going to be as he resettles the right leg beneath him. The point is to familiarize him with the signal to stop. Repeat the procedure, ideally, halting your horse at the very moment that his legs are crossed, at which point you can offer him a food reward. This is all it takes for many horses to remain in the legs-crossed position until told to walk on.

2 Squat in front of the horse, under his neck and a little to one side. (Note: This of course assumes that you have a very quiet horse and

In Brief

Starting Point: Horse can do a turn on the haunches in-hand.
End Goal: Horse crosses his forelegs.
Body Language: Move toward the horse with your body turned at a 45-degree angle toward his shoulder.
Voice Command: "Cross," or command of your choice.
Repetitions: Two or more times each step, depending on the horse.
Equipment: Halter, lead rope, whip.
Training Area: Arena or fenced-in area.
Preparation: Teach your horse to turn on his haunches in-hand.
To End the Exercise: Asking horse to step forward, halt, and assume the Statue (see p. 47).

you are working in a safe environment with no distractions and/or exterior commotion.) Touch his left shoulder blade with the fingertips of your right hand and then slide your right down the horse's left leg and pull it sideways so that it crosses the horse's right leg, which you may have to hold in place with your other hand. Ask the horse to hold this legs-crossed position by gently stroking the left leg, and maybe even hold it gently in place as you give him a treat. By using a food reward at this moment, many horses forget to step away with the right leg and so will stand with their legs crossed (as described in Step 1).

③ Now practice Step 2 until your horse begins to cross his legs merely from a light touch on his shoulder without you having to guide one leg over the other. When this begins to happen, assume an upright position at your horse's side and a little in front of him, and give the signal with your thumb or the knob of your whip.

④ Stand at a greater distance away from your horse, and touch his shoulder with only the very tip of the whip. Now accompany the crossing of *his* forelegs with the crossing of *your own* legs. The goal is for the crossing of your legs to become the signal for this trick.

⑤ Finally, vary the position in which you stand during this trick. First you stood to one side of the horse, facing him. Then you stood off to the side and slightly in front of him and began crossing your own legs when he crossed his. The more automatic this exercise becomes for your horse, the more you can move around him. This trick makes many people laugh—and the next one even more so.

Unrolling and Rolling-Up Carpet

Do you think it would amuse your horse to gradually nudge a rolled-up carpet, lay it out flat, and then roll it back up again the same way? Then have at it!

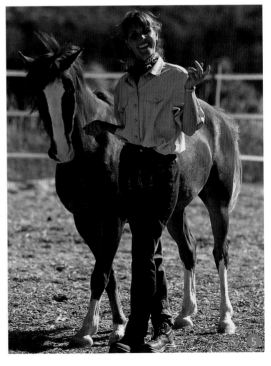

① First, the horse must have absolutely no fear of the carpet—whether rolled-up or laid out flat—and should be able to walk the length of it without hesitation. You can practice by unrolling your carpet runner and laying a strip of plastic along each side of it to "frame" it. If your horse will not walk down the carpet "aisle," remove the carpet and ask him to simply walk between the two strips of plastic until he feels secure. Widen the "aisle" between the plastic strips if necessary, gradually bringing them closer together with each repetition. Your horse should walk slowly and should halt on command at any time.

When your horse willingly Backs Up between the plastic strips, it confirms that he has understood and accepted the exercise. Put the carpet runner back between the two plastic strips and repeat this step until your horse walks the length of the carpet straight and under control. When he does, remove the plastic strips and do it a few more times.

② Now lay treat pieces about 6 inches apart along the length of the carpet so as your horse walks down the carpet runner he can "vacuum" up the tidbits. Repeat this exercise

In Brief

Starting Point: Horse willingly walks on a long piece of carpet runner.
End Goal: Horse unrolls and rolls up a long carpet runner.
Body Language: As in training your horse to Back Up (see p. 50), the trainer stands to the horse's left, facing his tail, and walks backward when the horse walks forward.
Voice Command: "Roll," or the command of your choice.
Repetitions: Two or more times each step, depending on the horse.
Equipment: Halter, lead rope, long narrow piece of carpet (runner) about 6½ feet long, two long strips of plastic about 6½ feet long.
Training Area: Arena or fenced-in area.
Preparation: Horse should be capable of a controlled walk, and a very slow walk in-hand.
To End the Exercise: Ask the horse to step forward, halt, and assume the Statue (see p. 47).

countless times. Your horse won't mind! Your goal is for him to always think, "I will find food on that carpet."

③ Now, roll up most of the carpet runner, with a treat tucked in every 4 inches or so. Leave about 20 inches of carpet unrolled on the ground with several treats visible, and hide a bit of food right under the edge of the roll. Lead your horse up to the carpet runner—he should immediately eat the treats that are lying out in the open, and then (we hope) he will notice the delicious aroma coming from under the edge of the roll and will try to get at its source. The only way he can reach the hidden treat is by nudging the edge of the carpet roll. If he does so, he has completed Step 3.

④ Some horses eat only the food that is readily visible and are not interested enough to find the rest. Or, they simply do not smell the other food and therefore do not look for it. The answer to this dilemma is to work on this trick right before your horse's morning or evening feeding—when he is hungry. This will speed things up! When your horse has made the first nudging move (at the end of Step 3) the next treat should be very close to the edge of the roll (in other words, place your food rewards pretty close together in the carpet roll). If your horse doesn't seem interested in nudging the carpet again, or if the next treat isn't apparent, put a tidbit right under the edge of the roll and encourage your horse to look for it and nudge the roll.

Your horse will soon grasp the exercise and unroll the whole carpet by nudging it along, exposing his treats along the way. Practice this trick with a large number of treats for the time being. Your horse will continue to be enthusiastic because it really pays for him to unroll this carpet runner! Once he seems very engaged in the trick itself, as well as the food rewards, gradually reduce the number of treats involved. You will find that your horse con-

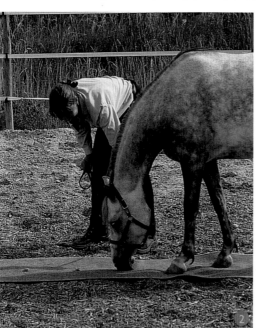

tinues to unroll the carpet with even stronger nudges as he gains in confidence.

5 Finally, the exercise should be so perfected that you do not have to roll treats up in the carpet. Instead, he is to nudge the carpet several times and receive a treat from your hand. Observe the feeding discipline discussed on p. 27. *You* determine when and where food rewards are given! Make the horse aware of the carpet roll with appropriate gestures so he proceeds to unroll it. Then, give him a treat. Repeat the process, decreasing the number of treats given until eventually you ask your horse to unroll the carpet without feeding him at all.

6 Once unrolling the carpet on cue has become an automatic response that does not require multiple food rewards, you can repeat Step 5, only ask the horse to nudge the roll in the *opposite* direction to roll the carpet back up. You now have the makings of a fun (and funny!) performance—perhaps unrolling a red carpet runner for the grand entrance of a friend riding her own horse...or how about a carpet unrolling race?

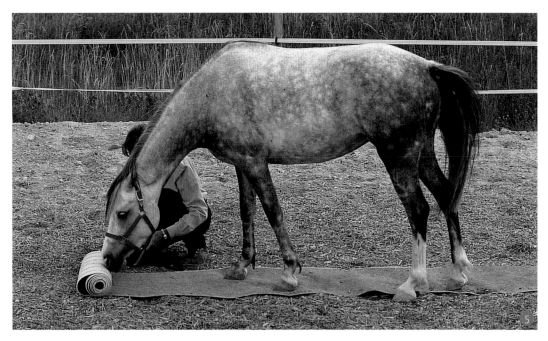

I once had a very amusing experience with Ben and this carpet trick. A trainer from New York (he specialized in Western riding) came to visit. His main interest was my husband Philippe Karl's training methods, which fascinated him. This trainer had a very good sense of humor, which inspired me to spontaneously cook up a little performance (unbeknownst to him!) as we stood along the edge of the indoor arena (Ben happened to be standing nearby). I turned to the fellow abruptly and asked, "Oh, are you not the man who called last week looking to purchase a carpet here in Provence?" The trainer looked at me with a puzzled expression and shook his head. My demeanor became even more earnest, and I went on, "Yes, yes—I remember the conversation exactly. You said you were coming here from New York particularly to shop for a carpet."

Now the poor man pointed to himself questioningly, and looked to the left and right as if perhaps I might mean one of the people who had accompanied him. I kept a straight face, but he had a thoroughly disoriented look on his! "Well, let me show you the carpet," I said.

I turned around and rummaged behind the riding boards that run along the lower half of the arena wall. (You would not believe how many toys and props I have hidden behind them. When my esteemed husband is not looking, I practice one crazy thing or another with my horses while he, with a contented expression, piaffes on horseback to the strains of Vivaldi.) I pulled out my rolled carpet runner, went out to where Ben stood in the arena, and put it down in front of him. Ben immediately began to unroll it, and we were both rewarded as the visiting trainer and his comrades got the gag and roared with laughter.

We spent much time then discussing the carpet's color and quality, before it was decided that the "precious" piece was far too expensive and our guest sadly declined to buy it. At that, Ben rolled the carpet up again! The moral of the story? Horse trainers from New York earn too little money to afford costly carpets from Provence. Pity!

Nudging and Pushing

If you decide to teach your horse the Nudging and Pushing trick, you must be comfortable with what the consequences may be. You must

be ready to control all your body movements so as not to provoke an unwanted Nudge or Push, and you must also be aware that if others work around your horse, they might unknowingly cue the trick—which could potentially cause problems. If you have any doubt in your mind regarding these issues, skip this trick altogether.

1 Begin by teaching your horse the Nudge. He should have a halter on to start, with a lead rope fastened to either side—one on the left and one on the right. Stand directly in front of him with your back to him, and hold a lead rope in each hand. Cross the ropes in front of your body and grasp their end with the opposite hand (imagine you are riding Western with split reins, using two hands). Direct the horse's nose to your back with a little pressure on the lead ropes. Some horses do not react at all at first, so try the exercise again, until the horse gives a slight little Nudge. Have a treat ready in your hand and give it to him right after he touches you. If your horse wants to evade or escape to the left, give a gentle tug on the right rope, and if he wants to go to the right, use the left rope.

2 If your horse moves to Nudge you of his own accord, give him a significant food reward with one hand behind your back. With so many treats on offer he will eventually want more, and may even beg with another Nudge: "Hey," he's saying, "I want more of that." And as a reward, he will get more!

3 Soon your horse will understand that every Nudge is rewarded. Now you need to incorporate a signal for the trick. Choose yours carefully, because it will impact how you move around your horse in the future. It can simply be turning your back toward the horse when directly in front of him, but remember, this

means that from now on you must always be careful to be to one side of your horse when you lead him, and never turn your back to reach for something when directly in front of him. Perhaps, in the future, you will even need to lead your horse with greater distance between you.

④ Once your horse understands the trick and the signal for it, it is very easy to transfer the Nudge on your back to become a Push on your bottom. Bend over in front of your horse—it would be very surprising if he did not get the idea to give you a Push with his nose. If he does not react, reattach the lead ropes and steer him toward your rear end.

⑤ Practice the trick with your horse at liberty. It is left to your preference as to whether you fall down after being Pushed, or run away, or perhaps you have your own funny ideas. Once your horse has thoroughly grasped the basic idea of Nudging and Pushing, it is very easy to steer him toward an object other than you—for example, a hat in your hands or a barrel. How you develop this trick into an act I leave to your imagination.

In Brief

Starting Point: Horse stands quietly directly behind the trainer.
End Goal: Horse gives the trainer a Push on her "hindquarters."
Body Language: Turn your back to the horse, bend over in front of him.
Voice Command: "Push," or command of your choice.
Repetitions: Two or more each step, depending on horse.
Equipment: Halter, two lead ropes.
Training Area: Arena or fenced-in area.
Preparation: The Statue (see p. 47).
To End the Exercise: Ask for the Statue.

Carrying Objects

It makes quite an impression when a horse picks up objects off the ground. Ben is an expert at picking up umbrellas, for example. He can also pick up and shake a pillow or a Racket Sack (see p. 58).

Before you begin training your horse to pick something up, shake it, and carry it, your horse should have learned many of the tricks in this book and he should find them fun for their own sake. I say this because in this trick, although we use treats to introduce the objects, there are no food rewards once your horse has picked an object up. If you want your horse to carry objects, he must first learn to hang on to them. But, if he stops midstride for a treat, he will open his mouth and let go of what he's carrying. So in this lesson, the horse must be satisfied with verbal praise and stroking.

① Begin by making your horse aware of an object lying on the ground. Do not use things that are easily chewed up or that you care about—like whips or riding gloves—because they might be damaged by your horse's teeth. It is best to begin with a lightweight object like a towel. Use a treat to coax your horse to lower his head and then put the treat directly on the towel. I recommend a handful of grain so that your horse must spend a long time looking for each kernel in the folds of the towel, which maybe leads to the towel ending up between his teeth a few times.

② Repeat. At some point your horse will get the idea of really putting the towel in his mouth. Praise him immediately with your voice and hands. When your horse has the towel in his mouth, ask him to lift his head. Again

In Brief

Starting Point: Horse stands still and quiet.
End Goal: Horse picks up object, shakes it, and/or carries it.
Body Language: Point to the object in question.
Voice Command: "Take it," or command of your choice.
Repetitions: Two or more times each step, depending on the horse.
Equipment: Halter, lead rope, towel, Racket Sack (see p. 58), pillow.
Training Area: Arena, fenced-in area, stall, cross-ties/grooming area.
Preparation: Leave an object within the horse's reach in his stall or the barn grooming area.
To End the Exercise: Ask for the Statue (see p. 47) and put away objects used for the trick.

praise him. Do not, under any circumstances, take the object out of the horse's mouth. He will probably let it fall out of his own accord after a very short time. Do not praise him when the object falls because what you want is for the horse to continue holding it. Simply begin the exercise again. As long as the horse holds on to the object, use your voice and hands to praise him generously. In my experience, horses quickly lose their enthusiasm for this game. Simply practice the trick for a short time again on another day.

③ During your next lesson, encourage the horse to move forward once he has picked up the towel, and practice with him carrying an object at the walk. Some horses do this as though it is nothing out of the ordinary, and others simply cannot walk while holding something in their mouth. If your horse has a hard time, simply go back to Step 2 before trying again to connect it to Step 3.

④ Now practice the exact same sequence using first an empty burlap sack, and once your horse has mastered picking that up, add a can filled with small stones, and then several more. Encourage your horse to shake the sack vigorously and make some noise—even so hard that a real racket ensues.

⑤ Gradually lengthen the time your horse walks while carrying the Racket Sack. Increase the number of times he shakes it.

⑥ Once your horse really understands the trick, work on asking him to let go of the object. You can initiate this by putting your thumb in his mouth as you do when you want him to open it for the bit. However, when your horse opens his mouth and lets go of the object, do not praise him! You do not want him to learn to actively drop the object. Associate the thumb in his mouth with a vocal command to "Drop it."

⑦ Once your horse picks up and carries an object, connect the exercise with coming

when you call him. First call him to you a couple times without the object, then with it.

The trick is perfect when the horse goes to an object, picks it up, and brings it back to you on cue. You may need an assistant when teaching him to go and get an object elsewhere in the arena, as at first he must be lured to it somehow. Then call him back to you. If your horse has trouble with the "departure" and the "return trip" (he wanders, or refuses to go or

My husband and I practice Coming when Called almost everyday with our horses. Philippe stands at one end of the arena and I stand at the other. Each of us is equipped with treats. Philippe calls the horse. The horse runs to him, and when he arrives and has been rewarded with food, I call him back. If a horse has trouble with this exercise initially, we simply decrease the distance between us.

come), then practice having him walk to your assistant and then back to you, using a longe line. (Note: You will need a second assistant for this exercise.) Begin with your horse next to you at Point A. The longe line should be attached to the horse's halter and extended across the arena to your first assistant. Upon your cue, your assistant urges the horse toward her (and the object) with pressure on the longe line. When the horse reaches her, he is praised and directed to pick up the object. At this point, your second assistant must take the longe line from your first assistant and bring it back to you, while you call your horse back to you. Again, you can help guide the horse back to you with pressure on the longe line.

8 When your horse understands Step 7 and performs it well, let him bring an object from one person to the other.

9 Change up the object your horse carries, shakes, or retrieves: Try a closed umbrella and a pillow, for example (two of Ben's favorites).

Under the Covers

I am currently teaching Anouk to pull a towel forward on her back while she is lying down. Ben already pulls a full-size comforter all the way over his head to "tuck himself in." (I've also taught him to place several stuffed animals exactly where he wants them for the "night.")

1 Before trying this trick, your horse must be taught to Lie Down (both "Awake" and "Asleep"—see pp. 115 and 126), and he must

have already learned to Carry Objects (see p. 89). Here we combine the two tricks. Let your horse Lie Down ("Awake"), position yourself behind his back and, with a treat, get him to turn his head toward you.

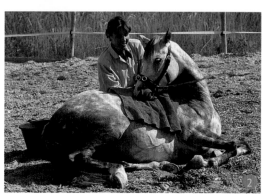

② From the same position, lay a large towel on your horse's back and, with a treat, get him to turn his head toward you so he becomes aware of the towel. Sprinkle some loose grain on the towel and again coax your horse to turn his head. He will begin to gather the bits of grain and will (most likely) get the towel between his teeth. When he does, praise him exuberantly.

③ As you repeat Step 2, your horse will soon recognize the objective (grab the towel between his teeth) and will probably pull the towel forward in the process. Much praise must be offered when this occurs. After many repetitions, switch the towel for a sheet that covers more of his body. Every tug that brings the sheet further forward should be met with praise.

④ Now, ask the horse to Lie Down ("Asleep") and try the trick from that position. Help him by letting him come up a little in order to grasp the sheet. Once he has it in his teeth, he should immediately lie down flat again. Eventually you should remove the halter and ask him to do this at liberty.

⑤ Exchange the sheet for a thick blanket or comforter, and make the "sleeping" act perfect by putting a pillow under your horse's head. Add stuffed animals to complete the picture!

"Unsaddled"

Ben and I have developed a funny act: I want to ride him, and he clearly says "No." Again and again I saddle up, but as I turn away (full of happy anticipation) he pulls the saddle pad and saddle off his own back. As with other tricks, before you teach your horse this one, you should consider the consequences: If, in the future, you always want to have an easy-to-saddle horse, avoid this exercise. Of course, my answer to this problem is to always saddle your horse (for real) from the left side, and only do the "Unsaddled" trick from the right side.

① Tie up or cross-tie your horse in his stall or in the barn's grooming area, and leave a towel within his reach. Move some distance away and observe your horse's actions. Many horses amuse themselves by nuzzling objects or throwing things that are within reach. If this is the case, praise your horse from your distant position, then go to him and feed him treats. If he has absolutely no interest in the towel, then try to find his special preference— for example, he might like a brush, currycomb, or hoof pick better. When you find one that works, praise him generously, and repeat.

② When the horse understands that he may grab the object, and does so willingly, switch objects. Your goal is for him to eventually grab a towel, because later you will substitute a saddle pad for it.

In Brief

Starting Point: Horse stands at liberty.
End Goal: Horse "untacks himself" by pulling the saddle off his own back.
Body Language: Tug on the saddle pad, jiggle the saddle.
Repetitions: Two or more times each step, depending on the horse.
Equipment: Halter, lead rope, towel, saddle pad, old saddle.
Training Area: Arena or fenced-in area.
Preparation: The Statue (see p. 47), Carrying Objects (see p. 89).
To End the Exercise: Ask the horse to walk on or assume the Statue.

What if Your Horse Gets "Grabby"?

Once you begin training your horse tricks, you will encounter everyday situations where you must carefully check your own habits and behavior, and when necessary, correct it. If your horse starts to grab at objects and you cannot use the behavior to further his carrying lessons (see p. 89), keep work areas tidy (do not leave things lying around) and do not let the horse play around in his stall or the barn's grooming area.

Remember, your horse cannot determine whether or not he is allowed to perform a trick or not in a complex situation. Scolding or punishing the horse in some situations will only undermine his motivation in others. What is required is the person must act deliberately at all times and be conscious of the everyday consequences of trick training.

③ Once your horse has learned to grab objects in the grooming area, change the training venue. (Remember: Keep tempting objects out of reach where tricks are not desired.)

④ In the arena or fenced-in area, stand to one side of your horse, at his croup, and bring his head toward his back by luring him with treats. Do this from both sides. Now, place a towel on his back and sprinkle grain on top of it. With your hand (and a treat, if necessary), lure your horse to the towel and the grain. He will likely pull the towel from his back at this first attempt to reach the grain. Praise him!

⑤ Switch the towel for a saddle pad, and again, sprinkle grain upon it. As before, praise your horse when he searches for food and pulls on the pad. At some point, stop putting treats on the pad and instead give your horse a food reward from your hand *after* he pulls the pad off his back. Connect a signal, like a soft tapping on his flank, with the horse turning his head toward his back and pulling off the pad. Gradually distance yourself from the horse and let him perform the exercise independently. At this point, you can "busy yourself" with picking the saddle up off the ground and—full of joyful anticipation—turn to place it on the horse's back. In the meantime, the saddle pad is already lying on the ground!

⑥ To increase the difficulty of the exercise, try it with an old saddle that can fall to the ground with no harm done. Use the same procedure as in Step 5. Your goal is for your horse to turn his head toward his back, grab the saddle with his teeth, and pull. For this he receives a food reward.

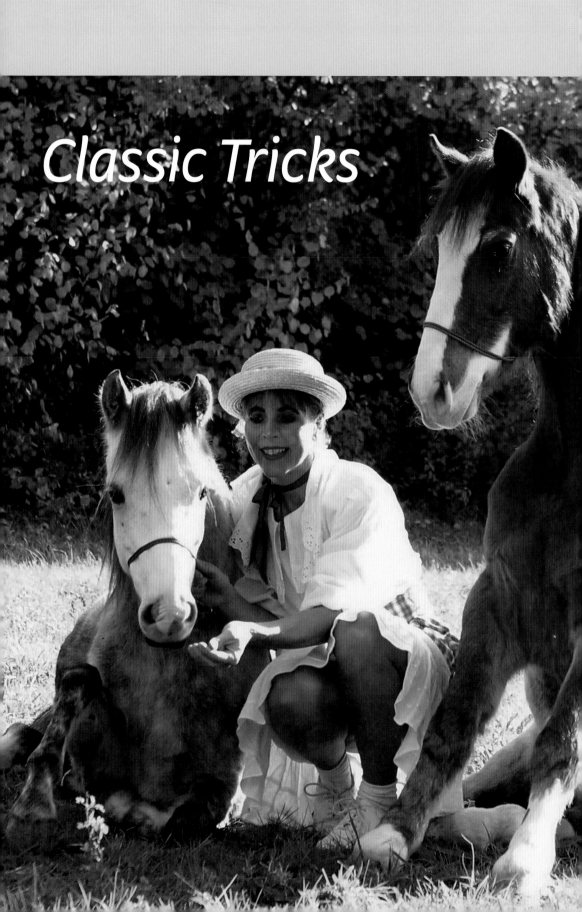

Classic Tricks

Classic Trick Basics

In this chapter I provide instructions for the horse tricks most of us are familiar with— ones we've seen on television, in movies, and in live performances. These are exercises that you surely expect to find in a book about trick training for horses, and therefore, I would like to accommodate you. I know that there are other resources available detailing these tricks, which I do recommend you read and view as well, if you want to explore this subject further.

There are two systems of progression from which the individual classic tricks can be developed.

System 1
Plié or One-Legged Bow, leads to ›
Kneeling, leads to ›
Lying Down, leads to ›
Sitting

System 2
One-Legged Bow, leads to ›
Lying Down, leads to ›
Sitting

For simplicity's sake I have explained all the tricks in this section from the left rein. Naturally, you can also work on the right side. Prior to working at liberty, I recommend using just a halter and lead rope or reins (if you need a connection on both sides of the horse's head) as this offers the gentlest connection and the one that is most friendly to the horse's mouth. If you attach reins to the halter, you can employ a stronger pull than you can with a bridle, if necessary. You can also use a longeing cavesson with side rings, if you prefer.

Plié

The Plié can be help you develop the One-Legged Bow (see p. 103), but it is not a prerequisite for that trick. I leave it to you to decide whether to work on Plié or the One-Legged Bow first.

Note: It is prudent, and better for the horse, to warm him up before starting any of the tricks that require stretching, such as Plié, particularly in the winter or during cold, rainy weather.

In Brief

Starting Point: Horse stands patiently.
End Goal: Horse stretches both front legs forward, steps both hind legs backward (parallel to one another), lowers his chest, and curves his head over his extended forelegs. The horse may lower his chest so far that it is within an inch of the ground.
Body Language: Stand at the horse's side, aligned with and at a 90-degree angle to his belly.
Voice Command: "Plié," or a command of your choice.
Repetitions: Two to three times each step, depending on the horse.
Equipment: Halter, set of reins, long whole carrots, whip.
Training Area: Arena or fenced-in area.
Preparation: The Statue (see p. 47).
To End the Exercise: Hold up the horse's head to keep him in the Statue position, drive him energetically forward, or summon the One-Legged Bow with a touch on the cannon bone of the leg that is to be bent (see p. 103).

You will be amazed at how many details are involved in this exercise and how much time it takes to train it properly.

1 *The Starting Point* Begin on the left rein and halt your horse. Stand at your horse's left side facing forward. Hold the halter with your left hand, while your right hand rests on your horse's withers. (This provides helpful support to your horse during the little balancing act that follows.) You are going to tell your horse to move his forelegs far apart—this is necessary because in the next step your horse has to lower his head between his forelegs, and he needs room to do that.

Bring your right foot forward between the horse's front hooves and tap the inside of the horse's left foot with it, right above the hoof, until your horse picks it up. "Pull" the left foot toward you with your right foot. Try to stay with the horse's leg, even if he pulls it away, so that you can immediately pull it back toward you. Encourage him to set down that left foot and put weight on it by pulling the horse's withers toward you. This shifts the horse's balance to the left onto his left hoof. Why do I suggest that you use your foot to manipulate the horse's foot, rather than your hand? Because you will use your hand when you practice the One-Legged Bow (see p. 103), and you should avoid having these two different tricks, and picking up the hoof for everyday cleaning, be too similar to one another.

If you have trouble getting your horse to react to your foot cue, press your right arm against the horse's belly so that he shifts his weight onto his right shoulder, then bend down and grasp his cannon with your left hand to suggest that he pick up his foot. Proceed as described earlier with your right foot "pulling" his left foot toward you. Reinforce this sequence with repetition.

2 In this step hold a long carrot in your right hand. Show your horse the carrot, but at first, do not let him take a bite. Instead, coax his head downward. Allow him to take his first bite when his muzzle is at pastern-level, and then another one when his muzzle is between his front hooves. Now reinforce this step with

What Does This Trick Have in Common with Riding?
Doing tricks well is exactly like riding well. I'm sure you are already aware of how many tiny details riding horses entails. Even when it is "only" circles or transitions or halting square, the details are what matter: tempo, balance, head/neck position, straightness, collection. You can't get the big picture right if you don't get the little things right first.

daily repetition, and introduce your vocal command, "Plié," so that your horse becomes accustomed to it.

③ Coax your horse's muzzle progressively further back between his legs. Continue to hold the carrot in your right hand, but now reach under his belly and only as far forward toward the forelegs as necessary. Encourage the horse to reach further back between his forelegs by holding the carrot perpendicular to his mouth so that he can feel it and touch it with his lips but cannot immediately bite off a piece.

If your horse does not readily follow you down and backward to where your right hand waits, have two carrots ready: one in your left hand and one in your right. With your left hand, lure the horse down to where your right hand can reach. Still having problems? Try again just before morning or evening feeding time, when your horse is at his hungriest. What? Your horse is never all that hungry? Re-think your feeding plan. (That is the short version of my at-least-15-minutes-long lecture on appropriate feeding to avoid fat bellies. Every one of my students can recite it from memory!)

④ The further back your horse follows your hand with his muzzle, the further back he must place his hind legs so that his chest can lower and his forelegs can stretch forward. Many repetitions will bring this about naturally.

⑤ *Stretching the Hind Legs* If Step 4 does not come about of its own accord, you must help develop it. Halt your horse and touch his left hind leg with your whip right above the coronary band, while, with your left hand on the halter, you give him a very minute signal to move backward. Your horse should *only* move the left hind leg backward. Repeat and reinforce this. Do the same thing with the other hind leg (you can reach across with your whip so you don't have to move to the other side of the horse) so that both hind legs are stretched out behind the horse. Come back to this step and repeat when necessary.

⑥ When your horse has fully grasped the idea of stretching his hind legs backward, connect this with the Plié movement. Hold the carrot in your left hand, between his front legs, to lure your horse's mouth progressively further

back, while touching his hind legs with the whip (held in your right hand). Repeat.

⑦ Condition your horse to lower himself into the Plié position by placing the palm of your hand on the point of his shoulder and pressing backward. Your horse will understand this signal if you connect it to something he already knows, so continue luring him backward with the carrot at the same time. The pressure on his shoulder, however, is only an interim signal. The actual signal for this trick should eventually be simply a touch with the whip under his belly. This allows you to work at a greater distance from the horse, which has a more elegant effect. (*Note:* A touch with the whip at the point of shoulder is too similar to the signal for Backing-Up or Spanish Walk.)

How does your hand on the horse's shoulder evolve into the ultimate cue for the Plié? You'll use both signals at once: tapping under

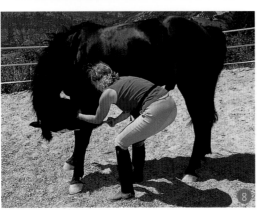

the belly with your whip while laying the flat of your left hand on the point of shoulder. Later, you can leave out the cue on the shoulder and only touch with the whip under the horse's belly. Working from a distance also means you should start working your horse at liberty (remove the halter).

⑧ *Remaining in Plié* To persuade your horse to "hold" this position, you can encourage him with food, which you will gradually decrease as time goes by. Crouch beside your horse at a 90-degree angle to his belly. As long as you are crouching and giving the whip or hand signal, your horse should remain in position. Reward him. Keep your horse down for only a short time at first and gradually lengthen the duration.

⑨ *Ending the Exercise* It is important that the horse rises on your command and that you anticipate him—in other words, if you sense he is about to get up, you should give him the cue to do so. Say, "And up!" and stand up yourself, then take a small step forward.

⑩ *Adjusting Head Position* How do you perfect the Plié and get your horse to hold his head freely over his outstretched forelegs? As you coax your horse's muzzle backward and downward with the carrot, tap him on his belly with it—you're saying: "Hello, the carrot is over here." When you have practiced this a few times and your horse reliably and consistently lowers his chest at a tap on his belly, use your right hand to give the signal, but hold the carrot in your left hand. This allows you to adjust the position of the carrot—and thus his head—over his outstretched forelegs.

Note: As a rule, this trick takes months to achieve.

How Plié Occurs Spontaneously

Spontaneous #1 I taught Tabea the One-Legged Bow (see p. 107) with a "leg rope" (a 12- to 15-foot soft rope with a loop in one end) before I taught her the Plié. One day while we were working she lowered her chest but "forgot" to bend one leg back. Instead she stretched both front legs and bowed over them with her head. Plié! I couldn't believe it—I had achieved a perfect Plié in no time at all! Naturally, Tabea was extravagantly praised and from that moment on I trained her in Plié and put the One-Legged Bow on the back burner (with the help of the leg rope, I knew I could easily get that trick back again). In general, you can adjust your training schedule in this way. If your horse offers a different or more difficult trick of his own accord, by all means accept the offering, and set aside what you *were* working on for the time being.

Spontaneous #2 My friend Michaela stretches her stallion Kino's front legs forward after she tightens the girth on her saddle so that the folds of skin under the girth smooth out. Many considerate riders do this. Kino became accustomed to stretching his back and body as this was being done (as horses like to do in the mornings after waking up). His stretch was the perfect Plié movement. Since Kino regularly made this movement, Michaela needed only to integrate a signal into the routine (press on the point of shoulder with her hand) and there was the Plié, always available on command. There is absolutely no reason not to take advantage of such fortuitous occurrences.

One-Legged Bow (without Leg Rope)

As mentioned earlier, whether you begin with the One-Legged Bow or the previously described Plié is your decision. The one furthers the other, and vice versa. They will probably require the same amount of time in either case. The difficult aspect of Plié is to get the horse to keep his head forward over his legs (see p. 101), whereas with the One-Legged Bow, getting the horse to independently bend and lower one foreleg can demand long and wearisome practice.

It does not matter whether you get your horse to go down on his left or right leg. That should depend entirely on which side you feel better and safer. If you wish, you can train your horse the One-Legged Bow from both sides right from the start. (Of course, for the sake of symmetry, your horse should master all the exercises on both sides.)

Whether to train this trick with or without the "leg rope" (a 12- to 15-foot soft rope with a loop in one end) is worth some advance consideration. Most horses are able to learn the One-Legged Bow without the leg rope. This is "friendlier" and less dangerous, but will most likely take you longer. I have great respect for students who want to work on the One-Legged Bow *au naturale*. Without a leg rope, nothing can be forced. I do choose to use one for some tricks because I am very knowledgeable about its use and because I want to reach my goals quickly (I have so many other ideas on which to work!) I feel I need to say that I am not certain that I can be 100 percent successful in accurately describing the correct use of the leg rope in this book so that you can safely use it. It would suit me best if you became familiar with the use of the leg rope in a trick training clinic or under an instructor's supervision, and then used my description in this book as a memory aide. (I do my best to explain the use of the leg rope with this trick on p. 107.)

1 Outfit your horse with a halter with reins attached. The reins should be shortened with a knot that rests just in front of the horse's withers, leaving no slack in the reins forward to where they attach to the halter, and creating a large loop at the tail end. Take an elastic bandage (a polo wrap works well) and bring it through this loop, then wrap the bandage around the horse's belly and tie it with a bow. This practical detail prevents the reins sliding down to the horse's ears during the steps to this trick. You can now reach for the reins at any time and know where they will be, which allows the trick to proceed with fewer distractions. (Note: You can also teach this trick with a lead rope attached to the halter and looped around the elastic bandage, as in some of the photos.)

2 *Starting Point* Stand on the horse's left side and face forward. Press against the horse's belly with your right elbow so that he shifts his weight to his right, while you reach down with your right hand and grasp his left cannon bone, picking up the foot.

What Does This Trick Have in Common with Riding?

In my opinion, agile, quick, hot-blooded horses serve to improve our riding, in general. Obedient, submissive, slow, cold-blooded horses and Warmbloods are not rebellious enough, which allows our riding to remain poor (they do not challenge us). Temperamental, difficult, or simply "hot" types of horses demand that you work with them in a way that is agreeable to them (speaks to their strengths and the way their mind works). This is something we must also take into account in trick training.

In Brief

Starting Point: Horse stands patiently.
End Goal: Horse bends one foreleg and lowers himself onto the cannon bone of that leg while the other foreleg is stretched out forward. The hind legs are stretched out backward and remain parallel to one another. The horse's chest is lowered but remains above the ground.
Body Language: Stand beside the horse facing the same direction; bend down to grasp the horse's leg and/or cue him, as necessary.
Voice Command: "Bow," or command of your choice.
Repetitions: Two or three times each step, as determined by the horse.
Equipment: Halter, lead rope, set of reins, elastic bandage (polo wrap), long whole carrots, whip.
Training Area: Arena or fenced-in area (soft footing is important).
Preparation: The Statue (see p. 47).
To End the Exercise: Raise the horse's head, drive him forward, ask for the Statue.

③ Hold the horse's bent leg up with your left hand while your right hand coaxes the horse's head down and back between his forelegs with a long carrot. Do not overdo it. Let your horse slowly become accustomed to the position. He should, bit by bit, lower himself progressively further.

④ Eventually, your horse will be so low to the ground the cannon bone you have been supporting will touch the ground. He may remain for a moment in this position, or maybe, surprised by his own actions, he will rush to get up. From here on out you should use the voice command. Consistent repetition brings

success. If you need to help your horse stretch out his hind legs, see my instructions for the Plié on p. 100.

5 *Remaining in the One-Legged Bow* Feed the horse treats as long as he stays down in the position. When he stands up, he does not get any more food. He will soon recognize the benefits of remaining in position and "hold it" longer.

6 *Adjusting Head Position* At this intermediate stage, your horse still holds his head between his forelegs. Proceed exactly as in Step 10 of the Plié (see p. 101). It is time to integrate the cue on his chest: Press with your hand against the point of shoulder, and as before, coax him down into the One-Legged Bow with a carrot. The signal on the chest keeps the horse down, and now feed him treats to one side of his body or between his bent leg and the one that is stretched forward.

7 Incorporate your whip signal (a touch on the horse's front cannon bone), and maybe even grasp his leg to help him, at first. After numerous repetitions, the horse should hold his leg up on his own. One may have to touch some horses on the cannon quite emphatically. You could also have begun with this step.

8 You now want your horse to react to your hand on the point of his shoulder and lower himself when you press on it, while with the whip in the other hand, you keep his one leg raised by touching the cannon bone. (Ultimately, this touch on the cannon bone will be the cue for the trick.)

9 *Remaining in the One-Legged Bow* If you would like your horse to remain in this position, you need to use food rewards to persuade him it is in his best interest. From your position beside the horse at his belly, step backward a bit toward his tail. Even with your adjusted position, the horse should remain in the One-Legged Bow as long as you continue

giving the whip signal. But, in the beginning, do not hold the cue for very long.

10 *To End the Exercise* It is important that the horse stands up on your command and that your command is given before the horse decides to change position of his own accord. Say "And up!" and stand up yourself, and take a small step forward.

Much time may have passed from the first time you attempted the One-Legged Bow and this point. Unfortunately, I cannot give a general timetable. There are horses that skip steps and others that require a great deal of time for each intermediate phase.

One-Legged Bow (with Leg Rope)

Advantages

> The trick is achieved more quickly.
> You do not have to adjust the horse's head position.
> The leg rope offers security and support, making it possible to train large, heavy horses how to do the One-Legged Bow.

Disadvantages

> Misuse and force are possible.
> Incorrect use leads to the horse's distrust of the trainer.
> I feel it requires supervision when first learning its use and training your horse with it.

When I describe the use of the leg rope in the following section,
I am addressing those trainers who will carefully consider its use, or who have already learned in a clinic or from an experienced trick trainer how to use it. My instructions are meant to serve as a review of the individual steps. I learned how to use the leg rope from Richard Hinrichs—a renowned in-hand trainer and creator of the bestselling DVD **Schooling Horses In-Hand** *(available from www.horseandriderbooks.com). I feel that owners of not-too-large-or-heavy horses with quiet, relaxed temperaments can give the leg rope technique a try. However, I recommend that owners of excessively large, high-strung, or difficult horses use this method only once a horse has mastered the basics of the trick and if they only need to polish and improve it. Read through all the steps before you begin. And again, I recommend that beginner trick trainers ask an experienced professional for in-person instruction and help.*

In Brief

Starting Point: Horse stands patiently.
End Goal: Horse bends one foreleg and lowers himself onto the cannon bone of that leg while the other foreleg is stretched out forward. The hind legs are stretched out backward and remain parallel to one another. The horse's chest is lowered but remains above the ground.
Body Language: Stand beside the horse facing the same direction; bend down to grasp the leg rope, as necessary.
Voice Command: "Bow," or command of your choice.
Repetitions: Two or three times each step, as determined by the horse.
Equipment: Halter, lead rope, set of reins, elastic bandage (polo wrap), long whole carrots, whip, gloves, leg rope (see p. 103), shipping boots (optional).
Training Area: Arena or fenced-in area (soft footing is important).
Preparation: The Statue (see p. 47).
To End the Exercise: Raise the horse's head, drive him forward, ask for the Statue.

1 Begin by setting up the halter, reins, and
elastic bandage (or polo wrap) as you did on
p. 103. For the first step in this variation, you
need an assistant. Both you and your assistant
should stand on the horse's left side; the assistant should hold him. Show your horse the
leg rope. Lay the leg rope on the ground around
the horse's left foreleg. Feed the horse a treat
low to the ground so that he sees the leg rope.
Gently dangle and drag the leg rope around
the horse's leg so that he becomes accustomed
to its movement and the feel of it. Pull the leg
rope up around the horse's fetlock and rub it
back and forth.

2 Have your assistant lead your horse forward
a few steps, halt him, and let him think. Repeat Steps 1 and 2 until you feel that your horse

has no problem with the leg rope being on or
near his leg, even when he is moving.

3 One end of the leg rope has a small loop
in it. When you feel your horse is ready,
place the leg rope around the horse's fetlock,
and pull the other end of the leg rope through
the loop. This creates a noose that you can
pull closed around the horse's fetlock and pull
closed. *Note*: In the steps ahead, *never* pick up
the horse's foot to "insert" it into the noose in
the leg rope; rather, the open leg rope should
always be placed around the leg as you've done
in this preliminary step, and then the noose
pulled closed.
   Gently move the leg rope around. Ask your
assistant to again lead your horse a few steps
forward and then halt him. Now drape the end
of the leg rope over the horse's back and lead
him forward again, on your own this time.
Make sure that the horse's movements are not
in any way hindered by the leg rope.

4 *Starting Point* For safety's sake I recommend beginner and novice trainers wear
gloves from this point on. Fasten the leg rope
around the horse's left foreleg as described in
Step 3. Begin with your horse at a halt and the
end of the leg rope in both your hands. Stand at

the horse's belly, facing forward. You will now practice getting your horse to lift his leg when you tug on the leg rope. Put gentle pressure on the leg rope and as soon as the horse responds by shifting the weight off the foot, hold it for just a moment, and release. Repeat.

5 Now take the free end of the leg rope and drape it—without any twists or bumps— across the horse's back. Reach under the horse's belly and bring the loose end back to your side. So the leg rope runs as follows: from the noose around the fetlock in a plumb line up to the horse's back, over the horse's back, down the offside, and back under the horse's belly to the near side where it should come just in front of the spot where the leg rope runs perpendicular up to the back. This is important because it gives the leg rope stability when you pull on it.

From this point on I like to call one part of this contraption the "leg rope" (the section that runs from the horse's foot up to his back) and the other part the "belly rope" (the part that is wrapped around the horse's barrel). Both sections will be used in the steps that follow.

6 Stand next to your horse on his left side at his belly. Face forward in the same direction as he is. Hold the free end of the leg rope in your left hand and grasp the leg rope about 20 inches above the fetlock. Hold the leg rope as you would a coffee cup or beer mug with your thumb pointing upward. Tug on the leg

rope. The horse should shift his weight off his left foot. If he does not, shift his balance to his right shoulder by pressing on his belly. If he does, immediately take up the slack in the leg rope. The horse's cannon bone should now be horizontal and the leg rope should hold it in this position. Repeat, conditioning your horse to be obedient to this signal: tug>lift foot>bend leg>wait with leg raised>lower leg>pause>repeat.

If you're still with me, great! I went back-and-forth as to how to write this as clearly and simply as possible.

7 One detail is very important: When your horse has bent his leg and you are holding the leg rope in your right hand, make sure that your hand is at the lowest possible point (just below the horse's girth line). If your hand is held too high (at the side of the horse's belly) your horse could, by fidgeting, pull your hand down. It is also important that your horse's lower leg remains horizontal to the ground— this ensures that when he lowers himself to the ground the impact isn't placed on the tip of his toe, which would stress his joints.

Watch how your horse reacts when you pull on the leg rope and hold his leg up. Difficult, anxious, or potentially explosive horses should be allowed to eat food out of a bucket or tub held by an assistant to help them adjust to holding their leg in the air for longer periods of time. If your horse begins to fidget, let go of the leg rope and start over. Many horses simply

need time to become accustomed to the sensation, so be satisfied to keep the leg up for only a few seconds, at first. Note: If you suspect your horse will fidget then protect him and yourself by putting shipping boots on his front legs, and even a pair on your legs (believe me, it works!) That way, you can, if necessary, let your horse fidget without fearing bruised shins.

8 If your horse rears or tries to break loose when the leg rope is used, work is proceeding too quickly. This can easily happen during clinics, which are often only a few days long. I try to offer my students many other ways to measure our "success" so that we do not feel compelled to finish a trick—in particular, this one—at any cost. The horse determines how long it takes to teach him a trick.

Just as you must have patience in teaching your horse a trick, your horse must learn to wait so that you have enough time to organize yourself at any point in the training process. Practice the gathering of the leg rope when the horse lifts his leg so frequently that the details become fluid (and safe) for you and your horse. Begin to employ the vocal command when you

pull on the leg rope. *Note:* I never use "Foot," or "Hoof," because I want my horse to distinguish between this trick and offering the hoof on command (for cleaning, for example).

9 *"Rocking"* Hold the leg rope in your right hand with its whole length coiled in loops. Your right hand also grasps the point where the "belly rope" and foot rope cross one another (see p. 109). With your left hand, grasp the reins, which are attached to the halter (see p. 97). Very quietly say "Ba-a-a-ack," and pull gently on the reins, as well as on the belly rope. Your horse should begin to shift backward, which you need to immediately stop by letting go of the reins and pushing your horse forward with your left hand on his shoulder. This step is called "rocking." Practice rocking calmly and for as long as it takes for your horse to trust himself to make progressively larger and deeper movements back-and-forth, until he gets to the point where his left cannon bone touches the ground.

10 If your horse does not move even the slightest amount, let him take several

---

What Does This Trick Have in Common with Riding?
If your horse frees himself from the leg rope by panicking or kicking, do not feel that all is lost. Calm, persistent repetition will assure your long-term success. It is not necessary that you adhere to the traditional notion that you must always, without fail, be the "leader," or the "winner," or otherwise enforce your will over the horse's. Patience and composure yield greater success.

This very important insight is just as valid in riding as it is in training this trick, and others.

steps backward and then lift his leg up and try again rocking again. If that does not help, pull strongly on the belly rope with your left hand. This is the main reason you should hold the leg rope in your right hand (as described in Step 6), because this way you are in better balance and can pull the rope diagonally to the side, while supporting yourself against the horse, if necessary. If this adjustment does not help, ask an assistant to feed your horse from the right side, helping to coax him progressively rearward and downward until he lowers himself to the ground.

As a last resort your assistant should feed the horse from between his forelegs. Unfortunately, this teaches the horse to reach his head back under his belly—a disadvantage of the regular training method (see p. 103) that you were hoping to avoid by using the leg rope. Once the horse understands what is wanted, you shouldn't have a problem adjusting his head position.

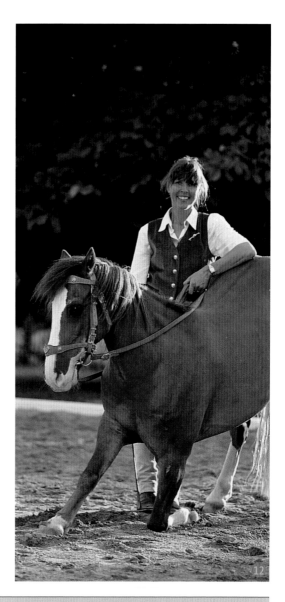

11 Your next goal is for your horse to remain in the One-Legged Bow for as long as you desire. Achieve this by feeding your horse treats as long as he remains in position.

12 Ultimately, your horse should stay in the One-Legged Bow even without treats. So, stop feeding him during the exercise and wait for the moment when he stands up of his own accord. Immediately bring him back down into position, wait a couple of seconds, and then rush him into his "normal" stance by standing up yourself and moving forward. In the same instant, say, "And up."

Keeping Them Different

Cleaning Feet
> In the barn aisle.
> Voice command is "Foot" or "Hoof."
> The trainer is positioned facing the horse's tail.
> The leg is stroked with the trainer's hand and the thumb encourages the horse's foot to be picked up.
> The horse's head is kept raised.

One-Legged Bow
> In the arena.
> Voice command is "Bow."
> The trainer faces the horse's head.
> The cannon bone is stroked with the whip.
> The horse is encouraged to lower himself with a rein signal and touch on the cannon bone.

13 Up to this point the leg rope was not only the tool that helped accomplish the trick, but also the signal for it. In the future you will work without the leg rope and so you will need another cue. Begin to replace pulling on the leg rope with touching the cannon bone with your whip.

14 The horse must learn to lower himself into the One-Legged Bow without the leg rope. Continue to use the belly rope (wrap the rope over the horse's back and bring it under his belly), but do not put the noose around his fetlock. Repeat Step 6. The horse should pick up his leg and hold it suspended when you touch his cannon bone with your whip. Practice and confirm this.

From now on, first give the signal on the cannon bone to lift the leg and then the signal to lower the body on the reins. After a few seconds, if necessary, pull the horse downward with the belly rope. At some point the horse will connect lifting his leg with lowering his body, and will lower himself into position at the touch signal on his cannon bone.

When I was teaching Tabea this trick, she responded better to the belly rope than to the reins. So, I wrapped the leg rope around her belly and touched the top of her cannon bone with the whip—at the pressure of the belly rope, she lowered herself into the One-Legged Bow. When she was doing this totally automatically, I removed the leg rope and she reacted to just the whip and voice signals.

What if...
...your horse lies down without being asked?
It can happen at any time during training this particular trick, with or without the leg rope, that your horse loses his balance and lies down. I believe in immediately profiting from accidental movements that may be difficult to train. If the horse unexpectedly lies down, I immediately give him treats, and I try to persuade him to remain lying down. You can only attempt this if you know how to safely keep a horse down (see p. 115). Remember, you can always come back to the One-Legged Bow later—take advantage of what may be offered by chance.

Kneeling

Kneeling is one step in the horse's natural process of lying down, which is why we value this exercise as a way to eventually persuade the horse to Lie Down on command. Although it is quite possible to ask a horse to Lie Down from the One-Legged Bow (see p. 103), doing it from the Kneel is far more comfortable. There are three ways to achieve Kneeling:

1 Kneeling from the One-Legged Bow

Sometimes this trick is offered by the horse, as I explain in detail next (see p. 114). If so, try to proceed that way, first—if you are successful, you will save time. If not, try beginning exactly as you did with the One-Legged Bow, and with the same equipment setup (see p. 103).

1 *Starting Point* From the left side of your horse, hold the halter with your left hand while your right hand controls the whip. Turn your body toward your horse's tail. By now, your horse has learned to remain in the One-Legged Bow until cued otherwise. Ask him for the One-Legged Bow, and then touch the extended cannon bone with your whip. Because your horse knows this signal and associates it with bending his leg, he very well may bend the extended leg and kneeling will result. If your horse does not respond, proceed with the next step.

2 If your horse has mastered the One-Legged Bow on one side, work on completing that trick on the other side. Practice to the left, then to the right, eventually switching from one to the other in rapid succession within a few seconds. Decrease the amount of time between left and right One-Legged Bows until it is only natural that your horse bends both knees momentarily.

If your horse does not respond to light touching on his extended leg, you can try to manually move the stretched leg sideways-and-backward so the leg bends. With this step, you need an assistant to hold your horse or manipulate the leg. When you have done it for him several times, your horse will get the idea.

3 Keep your horse's chest from getting too low in the Kneeling position with a gentle upward tug on the reins knotted around the horse's neck (see p. 103). With "half-halts," urge the horse to hold his head and neck up. This can also later be a signal to the horse that he should rise from the lying down position, or not go down in the first place. It may be necessary to let someone help you by holding the horse's head up or feeding him to keep him in an upright position.

In Brief

Starting Point: Horse stands patiently.
End Goal: Horse Kneels—both forelegs are bent at a right angle. The hind legs are forward under the belly, open and parallel to one another. The horse's head is free and held clearly above the ground.
Body Language: Lower your upper body, and turn toward the horse's tail.
Voice Command: "Kneel," or command of your choice.
Repetitions: Two or three times each step, or as determined by the horse.
Equipment: Halter, lead rope, reins, whip.
Training Area: Arena or fenced-in area.
Preparation: One-Legged Bow, preferably to both sides.
To End the Exercise: Hold the horse's head up, drive him forward, tell him "Whoa, halt."

2 Kneeling Spontaneously

① It is worthwhile to see whether your horse
will spontaneously bend both knees when
you very suddenly, but neither timidly nor
roughly, touch him (with the whip) on both
front cannon bones at the same time. Hold
him firmly at the halter so that he does not try
to escape. Bring his head forward and down.
Step far to the side because the horse could,
as a reflex, strike out, although this is unlikely.
If your horse does not respond promptly with
his playful instincts and Kneel, then there is
little point in trying to teach the trick from
this angle.

The spontaneous Kneel usually only works
with very sensitive or very green horses, or
those that play with others a great deal. In play,
pasturemates may bite or strike at each other,
with one going so far as to bend his knees to
protect himself before regaining his feet and
retaliating.

3 "Dancing" into the Kneel

Tabea has necessitated I develop a third way to
teach the Kneel, as she goes far too deep when
asked to perform the One-Legged Bow.

① *Starting Point* Stand next to the horse and
hold him close to the halter in a firm manner so he cannot escape by yielding away from
you. I recommend working on this exercise beside the fence or wall so your horse has a lateral
boundary.

② Touch the inside leg and the horse should
lift it, as when teaching the One-Legged
Bow (see p. 103).

③ Touch the other leg, with the same goal
in mind—the horse should lift it. Proceed
with an air of complete calm, because your
horse should not act out of a panic reflex but
because he understands the exercise.
Practice alternate lifting of the front legs.

④ Begin to switch rapidly, touching first
one leg then the other so that your horse
"dances" from leg to leg. Practice this for several days.

⑤ Stand beside your horse and ask him to lower his head forward and down. You want to ask for this movement somewhat abruptly in combination with the alternating touches on his forelegs so that your horse bends both legs at the same time, thereby going into the Kneeling position.

⑥ You may need an assistant when using this method. She prevents the horse from evading backward. *Forward* movement is an integral detail in this trick. In order to be able to Kneel, a horse must shift his weight forward from behind (from back to front).

Remaining in Position and Standing Back Up

One way or another you have managed to teach your horse to Kneel. If your horse quickly regains his feet, you need to work on persuading him to remain in the Kneeling position. As your horse is Kneeling, take the whip into your left hand, turn so you face the same direction as your horse, and put your right hand on his back as a signal for him to remain in place. In time, with enough repetition, this should work. If not, feed your horse treats from a bucket or tub while he is in the Kneeling position.

Next, your horse should learn to stand up on the command "And up!" Speak these words while at the same time you move abruptly upward yourself and take one step forward. Your horse will either leap up, or he will extend one foreleg and then the other out in front of him as he works his way back to his feet. Both are okay. If he has no idea what he is supposed to do, grasp the halter with your left hand, give a light tugging signal to move forward, and, at the same time, give a touching signal at the croup with your whip.

Lying Down "Upright" (or "Awake")

The first question you face here is whether or not your horse lies down with or without the help of the leg rope (see p. 103). If you succeeded in teaching the One-Legged Bow without the leg rope, then you should try to continue without it.

Lying Down from the Roll

"Oh, no..." I can hear my fellow trick trainers moan. Countless students have showed me how they trained their horse to Lie Down on command this way. I, too, have used this method in the past—with Tabea, as she's a bit sensitive and needs to be trained carefully. Training Lying Down from a roll is helpful for difficult or dominant horses, or those that are large and/or heavy. It is a particularly successful way to teach horses that will do anything for food.

Keeping Them Different

One-Legged Bow
> *Person stands parallel to the horse and faces forward.*
> *Whip touches one leg from behind.*
> *Vocal command is "Bow."*
> *To ask the horse to remain in position, take a small step backward.*

Kneeling
> *Person stands parallel to the horse and faces his tail.*
> *Whip touches one or two legs, depending on method.*
> *Vocal command is "Kneel."*
> *To ask the horse to remain in position, turn and place a hand on the horse's back.*

1 *Starting Point* Your horse, when given the opportunity, regularly and gladly rolls after a workout. (If not, this method of teaching a horse to Lie Down is not an option for you.) Begin to incorporate the following ritual after your horse's workout: Accompany him as he rolls, standing at a distance of 6 to 10 feet away, and observe his movement. How much space does he need? Where must you stand if you want to end up very close to him as he finishes? (Naturally you must position yourself at the front of the horse, always ready to increase the distance between you, if necessary.) You need to communicate to your horse, "From now on I will always be nearby when you roll after working." Soon, your horse will become accustomed to this.

Follow the horse wherever he goes prior to rolling; follow his turns, bend down toward the ground yourself, and simulate the horse by pawing the ground with your foot (this can help encourage him to lie down and roll). After several days later, from a good distance away, offer him a treat with your arm outstretched to its full length, at the exact moment he lays down to roll. Perhaps he will ignore you at first and roll immediately rather than pausing to consider the food reward. That is why you must keep your distance. But, maybe you will have a chance to feed him after he has rolled, while he is still lying on the ground. If not, do not give up. Just keep repeating this sequence again and again. It will all fall into place soon.

2 Once you have succeeded in feeding your horse treats immediately after he has rolled, keep feeding him for as long as he remains down. Do not limit the amount of food you give him. Of course, as soon as he stands up, he should no longer receive treats.

3 Soon your horse will look for a treat as soon as he goes down, even before he rolls. Your horse will enjoy being fed and may find it quite amusing to be rewarded with food—and quite a lot of it—for doing something that he enjoys and fully intended to do anyway! (Most likely this is the first and only time he's experienced such a thing.) Work on this over several days.

In Brief

Starting Point: Horse standing patiently.
End Goal: Two stages: Horse Lying Down "Upright" (or "Awake")—that is, with his body on the ground, his legs folded under his belly, and his head and neck up and alert; and horse Lying Down "Flat" (or "Asleep") with his whole body stretched upon the ground, including his head and neck.
Body Language: Bending down, "pawing" with your own foot, "making yourself small."
Voice Command: "Down," or the command of your choice.
Repetitions: Two or three times each step, depending on the horse.
Equipment: Halter, lead rope, reins, elastic bandage (or polo wrap), gloves, whip.
Training Area: Arena or fenced-in area with soft footing and a lot of space around the horse.
Preparation: One-Legged Bow (see p. 103) or Kneeling (see p. 113).
To End the Exercise: Drive the horse up and forward into walk or trot, hold his head up.

④ Soon your horse will Lie Down and won't even bother to roll—as he is too busy waiting for "breakfast in bed"! Do you know who is happiest at this moment? *Both* of you! Both of you are thinking, "I have gotten what I want."

⑤ When your horse starts to Lie Down frequently in your presence, but does not roll, get closer to him and begin to integrate a signal into the process. I use a touch of the whip on the underside of the horse's belly.

⑥ Eventually, gradually, summon the trick with this cue. As performance of the trick becomes more consistent and reliable, you can add other signals—a touch on the hind cannon bones if the horse needs to be reminded to step under and bend at the hocks, or on the front cannon bones to convey the same thing (bending at the knees).

What if...
...I cannot get my horse to Lie Down on cue via a roll?
If, after many attempts, you are stuck in the stage where your horse circles around for ages without Lying Down, or continuously goes off to find another spot, then move on to the other methods I discuss, including using the leg rope (see p. 119) or beginning with the One-Legged Bow (see p. 118).

Lying Down using a leg rope.

Tabea learned Lying Down from a mixed bag of methods—first from the roll, then with a leg rope, and also from the One-Legged Bow. Only (oh, horrors!) she liked to get in a roll, whichever method we were using, and at that point it became dangerous. I could not stop her from rolling by having her Lie Down "Flat" (see p. 126) because I could not in any way use the reins to control her. She was highly explosive, and using the reins would have pushed unnecessary buttons. So, I just let her roll, and then, as described in Step 2, I kept her down with treats.

Lying Down "Upright" (or "Awake") from the One-Legged Bow

This process works for only a very few animals, but for the sake of encouraging the horse's participation and free will, you should give it a sufficiently long try.

1 *Starting Point* Prepare your horse with a halter and a set of reins tied around his neck, plus an elastic bandage around his barrel (the same equipment as described on p. 103). Stand on his right side and offer him treats at the girth line so that he has to bend his neck around. Reinforce this step through repetition. Now add a touch of the whip at the girth when you offer treats. The horse learns that whenever you give this signal, he will get a food reward.

2 Switch to the left side, reach over the horse's back with your right arm, tap him on the right side of his belly, and then offer him treats when responds correctly. If your horse is very tall, use a mounting block or another stable object on which to stand. If you don't have a mounting block, I urge you to get one. You should not mount your tall horse (well, any size horse, really) from the ground. A mounting block is better for your horse's back, your joints, and your saddle.

3 Now, ask your horse to perform the One-Legged Bow several times in a row, and then, right before he lowers himself again, bend his neck to the right. Help your horse decide to bend his neck on command by having an assistant stand at the horse's right side offering treats with an outstretched arm.

4 *"Rocking"* When your horse can do Step 3, you can revisit the "rocking" technique you used in the One-Legged Bow (see p. 110). This

(see p. 126); (see p. 103); (see p. 110)

What if ...
...I cannot control on which side my horse Lies Down?
This is the reason why many trick trainers avoid this method of teaching a horse to Lie Down: It is difficult to control on which side the horse will go down. Most likely, your horse Lies Down with his legs toward you because he instinctively does not want you behind him in his "blind spot." Is it really necessary to control on which side he Lies Down? Not at first, because if, through numerous repetitions, your horse lies down calmly (whichever side he does so), then at least you are not in danger. Critics are justified in that you do eventually need the ability to summon the exercise on cue, on either side. The goal is that you can, with the appropriate signal, ask your horse to Lie Down whenever and wherever you choose. If you can't determine on which side he Lies Down, it will become noticeable eventually. If you feel you must have this degree of control from the beginning, then try the other methods I've offered on pp. 115 and 119.

plays with your horse's balance—he bends his hocks during the changes of balance, and in doing so notices that it is not so terrible. Ultimately, he "plops" to the ground and because of the neck-bending steps that preceded this, he will probably land with his belly toward you.

⑤ You can also go down into the Kneel first as an intermediate step (tap with the whip on the front of the horse's extended front cannon bone to ask for the Kneel—see p. 113). Bend the horse to the right and let him remain Kneeling but with a bend. Your horse will begin rocking on cue (see Step 4) and eventually this leads to him going all the way down.

Why Is Lying Down So difficult for the Horse?

Doesn't the horse Lie Down of his own accord several times within the space of 24 hours? In my opinion, the involvement of a human being makes the exercise difficult. Although Lying Down is something about which the horse feels confident, consciously performing such an otherwise everyday, instinctive movement is unusual. To begin with, he must assess what the person is doing there at his side or behind his back. Going down leaves him in a vulnerable position—he is at a great disadvantage should he be attacked by a predator. Perhaps, also, the horse is "worried" about the trainer (afraid of stepping on her and/or knocking her down). It is this way with Ben—I am very familiar with a horse's capability for considerate actions. However, even a very thoughtful and considerate horse cannot determine where we are when we are in his "blind spot."

Because of these factors, it is important to:
> *Make the Lying Down on cue process understandable for the horse.*
> *Give the horse time to consider and judge the situation.*
> *Arrange the process in such a way that the horse sees it in a positive light (that is, it is fun, not work). Only in that way can he accept the trick and be prepared to perform it on cue in the future.*

Most trainers would say this involves "earning the horse's trust." Lying Down on cue and the training challenges it poses are, for me, recurring proof that it is not enough just to have a horse fit and physically able to do something, you must also get him to understand and accept the task.

What if...

...my horse, despite careful preparation, does not let me bend his head and neck around?
I answer this question assuming that you already practice preparatory groundwork frequently enough that your horse knows what to do (see p. 42). Some horses, however, brace the neck or the poll, and when using only a halter, the trainer is not in a position to appropriately influence the situation. Use a bridle with a full-cheek snaffle (this bit cannot be pulled through the horse's mouth and is a more effective aid).

Lying Down "Upright" (or "Awake") with the Leg Rope

1 The ideal way to use this method is to ask the horse to go from the One-Legged Bow to the Kneel, and from there into Lying Down. Revisit my instructions for using the leg rope beginning on p. 107, and again practice the transition from the One-Legged Bow to Kneeling, as described on p. 113.

2 Train the horse to bend his neck 90 degrees, as described on p. 118. At first use treats to coax the horse to bend to both sides; then bend the neck using the reins attached to the halter.

3 Stand on the horse's left side, ask him to perform the One-Legged Bow using the leg rope, and after he has lowered himself, bend him away from you to the right. If the horse rises from the position, stroke him and repeat what you just did. Gradually increase the bend. Whenever he rises of his own accord, lead him

back into the One-Legged Bow and try again, perhaps for a bit longer this time.

Remember, what is important is that your horse understands you and accepts the exercise. So, do not let force creep in (which is possible when using the leg rope). Rather, win him over with your loving but persistent, deliberate repetitions. Eventually your horse will stay down for a longer time, and maybe he will offer to Lie Down on his own. If not, rock him toward you a bit (see p. 118) as you did when teaching him the One-Legged Bow. Watch his hocks for any sign that he may be "thinking" about Lying Down (I call this the hocks "going soft"). Praise extravagantly if you see this.

4 Stand beside your horse, facing his tail, and tap/touch the back of his hind legs with the whip. At the same time, give the tiniest signal to go forward on the halter. If your horse lifts a hind foot and puts it forward just a bit, he has understood. If not, grasp the hoof after you have tapped/touched it and bring it forward manually. Do the same thing on the other side and practice obedience to the whip cue.

What Does This Trick Have in Common with Riding?

You have to make the process understandable for the horse (for example, trotting cavalletti before jumping a cross-rail, or teaching shoulder-in in-hand before trying it under saddle). Set up training sessions in such a way that the horse views the challenge in a positive light (stop every now and then and generously reward him with voice, hands, and food), so that, as a result, he accepts the trick, volunteers to do it, and thereby confirms, "I understand what you want and I am highly motivated." Ultimately, he will have a lot of fun with this trick. If, during the process, you have shown your own pleasure and enthusiasm, then your horse will "smile" along with you.

5 Combine Step 4 with the One-Legged
Bow from Step 3. You want your horse to
be "soft in the hocks" when he is in the
One-Legged Bow. Lifting the hind feet and
bringing them forward is a step toward that.
Eventually your horse will dare to bend his
legs progressively more until he falls gently
to the ground. If you have a horse that lacks
confidence, lean into him with your knee (the
one closest to him) as he begins to Lie Down.
This "support" gives him the confidence he
needs to go ahead and do it. With an agile
horse that reacts less tentatively, you should
allow sufficient space for him to go down by
moving out of his way.

6 When your horse lies all the way down on
the ground, four different reactions could
result.

First: He may remain in the "Upright" or
"Awake" position with his head and neck up.
Feed him generously and show your elation. (I
know I do not need to mention that last bit, as
by now you will do it anyway!)

Second: He may Lie Down "Flat" or "Asleep"
with his neck stretched out and his head on
the ground. No matter—even though you are
working on the first phase of the Lying Down
trick, you'll want him to Lie Down "Flat" eventually, so praise him and offer him treats as he
remains in that position.

Third: He gets right back on his feet immediately (refrain from praising him).

Fourth: He immediately begins to roll (stay
clear of his legs and mind the leg rope doesn't
get tangled).

What if....
....my horse "tips over" his shoulder instead of bending his hocks to go down correctly and comfortably?
Practice rocking for a longer time (see p.118), and while doing it, leave the horse's neck straight (that is, do not ask him to bend right or left). Practice rocking on four legs, on three legs with the leg rope raising one front leg in preparation for the One-Legged Bow, and finally, in the One-Legged Bow itself. Avoid "pulling" your horse down in front because that is the cause of this error.

What if...
...my horse immediately wants to roll?
Your horse may not roll in close proximity to you. And, if used the Lying Down from the Roll method (see p. 115), then you need to reestablish a reward system before he has a chance to roll in order to confirm the trick. In other scenarios, prevent him from rolling after he Lies Down on cue in the following ways:

With temperamental, "explosive" horses:
Immediately step away and use the same process as described in the section about using the horse's instinct to roll as an introduction to Lying Down.

With calm, unflappable horses:
In order to roll, the horse must gather momentum, in this case by briefly turning to one side. Prevent this turn in order to prevent the roll. If you are on the horse's left, for example, with him Lying Down facing away from you, use the reins attached to the halter so that the right rein is on his neck and the left rein is moved away from his neck (an "opening" rein). Bring both hands energetically to the left so that the horse lies down flat. Once the horse is lying flat, hold his head firmly on the ground by energetically pulling on the left rein. If the horse cannot move his head he cannot roll. Only when he is no longer attempting to roll should you loosen the reins and give him treats while he remains Lying Down.

What if.....
....the horse immediately jumps back up on his feet?

With temperamental, "explosive" horses:
As always, with this kind of horse you have no option but time and patience. You can also try what I did with my mare Monodie: We worked on perfect, instantaneous obedience to the "halt" command, so that the "freeze" was effective, even when she was lying on the ground.

With calm, unflappable horses:
Once your horse has lain down, instantly bend his neck to the right with a wide, opening rein aid so that his muzzle touches his belly, or coax him into this position with food. Do not force anything; repetition will help you.

Remaining in the Lying Down Position

1. Begin as I have mentioned already—try to keep your horse down with food. Squat behind him and reach over his back to feed him treats so he bends his neck to touch his belly. When a horse stands up, he uses his neck, straightening it and extending it up in the air. So, bending him around to one side and feeding him treats encourages your horse to stay on the ground.

2. Before your horse climbs back to his feet of his own accord, step back from his side and give him the command, "And up!" He should learn that when you are at his side he should remain on the ground, but when you move away, he may get up.

3. With repetition you will get to the point where your horse remains on the ground

for longer periods of time. Feed him "as much as he can take." Because of the treats, your horse will gladly remain Lying Down. Even my skittish Tabea understands this and values her time of rest and food rewards.

④ Once your horse thoroughly understands the rules of the trick and has come to the point where he remains lying down for however long you please, take the whip and stroke him all over with it, as you did in the Statue (see p. 47).

⑤ As you did with the Statue, gradually increase the distance between you and the horse, and let him get up only when given the command "And Up!"

⑥ Begin to walk around the horse and feed him from the other side. Never feed from the front because that is where he extends his legs prior to standing up, and he could step (painfully) on you. Note: I never use pressure to keep the horse down on the ground, whether he is lying flat or upright. Time works for me. Force is absolutely not necessary; it is only harmful.

In the future, your horse will distinguish the command to Lie Down from the directive to Kneel because of:
> *Different voice commands.*
> *Different whip cues.*
> *In Kneeling you use the reins to keep the horse's neck straight and his head up, whereas for Lying Down you bend his neck around toward his belly.*

Lying Down "Flat" (or "Asleep")

① *Starting Point* Ask your horse to Lie Down "Flat" only after he has mastered Lying Down "Upright" because by then lying flat is just a minor matter. The steps to this trick correspond to the methods I described for stop-

ping a horse from jumping up and preventing him from rolling (see pp. 123 and 124). Prepare your horse as before in a halter with reins attached. However, the reins should not be knotted this time so they can be used to their full length. Stand behind your horse (already Lying Down in the "Upright" or "Awake" position) on his left side, for example, and make contact on the reins. Bend the horse's neck (to the right, in this example) with your hands spread wide apart. On the left rein pull gently downward in the direction of the ground. As you do that the right rein comes to lie on the horse's neck. Your horse will follow your movement and bring his head and neck down to the ground. Feed him for as long has he remains lying flat on the ground.

② If your horse jumps up, do not hold on. Instead, try again and depend on your horse growing accustomed to the exercise. With Anouk I experienced how uncertain (insecure) a horse can be when learning this trick, but also how much he will improve from day to day if you allow enough time for gradually attaining success. It is not always necessary to change your tactics or rely on special tools. More often, you just need time and patience.

From Lying Down "Flat" to Lying Down "Upright"

Some horses do not want to Lie Down "Upright" (see p. 115) and instead Lie Down "Flat," and others "throw" themselves flat on the ground right from the One-Legged Bow. If your horse is one of these, reward him in that position, regardless, and remain calm. He may, of his own accord, bring his head and neck up without getting all the way to his feet. But, that will probably not be what happens. Let's assume that you are standing on your horse's left side and your horse is Lying Down with his back toward you. Urge him upright with the reins (attached to either side of the halter—see p. 97). The left rein should be against the horse's neck (which is flat on the ground) and the right rein should be an opening rein held away from his neck. Gently nudge him at the side of his belly with your toe to initiate some movement. If the horse begins to rise, bend his neck strongly to the right to prevent him from getting all the way up (see p. 124).

When I taught Tabea to Lie Down with the leg rope from the One-Legged Bow, she would immediately lie down flat on her side. I couldn't interfere with this because she can be a bit excitable, which forces me to remain

In Brief

Starting Point: Horse Lying Down "Upright."
End Goal: Horse Lying Down "Flat."
Body Language: Calm, standing or squatting at the horse's side, using reins as necessary.
Voice Command: "Flat," or a command of your choice.
Repetitions: Two or three times each step, or as determined by the horse.
Equipment: Halter, lead rope, set of reins, elastic band (polo wrap), gloves, whip, leg rope (if necessary).
Training Area: Arena or fenced-in area with soft footing and lots of room around the horse.
Preparation: Lying Down "Upright" (or "Awake").
To End the Exercise: Use rein aids to energetically urge the horse to lie with his head and neck elevated.

very calm. I cannot use the reins to bring her into the "Upright" position. So, I wait. When I have an assistant on hand, I remain behind her while my assistant uses treats to coax her into position.

Sitting

Before starting this trick, your horse should be warmed-up properly. You also need appropriate footing. It should be soft enough to be comfortable but solid enough that the horse's hooves do not slip.

1 *Starting Point* Your horse should have mastered Lying Down "Upright" and you should be able to walk around your horse (when he is in that position) without him moving. In the first phase of the Sitting trick, use your hands to guide the horse's front legs forward. Say he is lying on his left side with his legs facing right. Squat on his right side, facing his legs, giving him treats. Slowly guide the right leg forward and rest it before him in an arc. Stroke the leg continuously and keep feeding your horse. After a while, walk away, and with your voice, encourage your horse to stand up. Repeat this sequence until it is confirmed.

In Brief:

Starting Point: Horse Lying Down "Upright"
End Goal: Horse sits on his hind end with both forelegs centered between his hind legs.
Body Language: From squat to standing at the horse's shoulder.
Voice Command: "Sit," or the command of your choice.
Repetitions: Two or three times, as determined by the horse.
Equipment: Halter, lead rope, set of reins, elastic band (polo wrap), whip.
Preparation: Lying Down "Upright" calmly and for as long as desired by trainer.
Training area: Arena or fenced-in area with soft but firm footing.
To End the Exercise: Ask horse to Lie Down "Flat," energetically drive him forward and up.

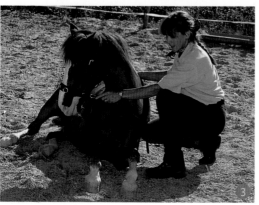

2 Repeat Step 1, but this time, pull the other leg forward, too, also stroking it with your hand while you feed your horse treats. Remember not to limit the amount of food but rather keep feeding him for as long as he remains calmly in position. As before, move away from your horse so that he may get up on your command.

3 Once your horse has learned to stay in position with this forelegs out in front of him, you can ask him to stretch his legs forward on his own by connecting a cue (I use a gentle touch on his forelegs or shoulder) with Step 2. Repeat until you no longer move the legs yourself, but instead your horse stretches them out when he feels the signal.

4 Now ask your horse to Lie Down "Flat" from the legs-stretched-forward position. To do this, stand on his left at the withers, bend his neck right, and as you did earlier from the

Lying Down "Upright" position (see p. 126), use the reins to lay him down flat. Then move away and say, "And up!" so he rises.

⑤ Once your horse remains in position with his legs stretched out in front of him for as long as you desire, and only gets up when you give him the room and command to do so, then you can begin to "feed him high." With your horse in the Lying Down "Upright" position, ask him to stretch his forelegs out before him. Position yourself on your horse's left side (for example) at his head, offer him food with your left hand, and cluck softly so that he begins to think about moving. If he makes a very small shifting movement to lever himself upward, reward it immediately by feeding him again with your hand held low. Repeat and reinforce this.

Maybe your horse will, of his own accord, amplify his attempts to alter his position. If not, encourage him to do so by holding your (feeding) hand progressively higher. In accordance, your horse will lift himself progressively higher so he can reach the food.

⑥ It may be necessary to work with an assistant. If you have one, you can stand near your horse's withers, holding the reins wide apart, while your helper is at his head and ready to give him treats. Quietly ask your horse

to lever himself up from the Lying Down position with upward pressure on the reins and maybe even a nudge on his shoulder with your knee. As soon as he begins to lever his front end up, stop him very gently with the reins. You only want to give him the idea; you don't want to force it. He should trust himself to try to understand the new trick.

7 If possible, end each attempt by having your horse Lie Down "Flat" as in Step 4. This is not absolutely necessary, but it increases the horse's understanding that he should stay on the ground for as long as you want him to remain there.

8 Halting Instantaneously on Command

If your horse scrambles to his feet, keep trying. Your horse should try to lift his front end *just a little bit*. At first, the movement may not be very noticeable. But with time and praise, your horse will gradually attempt more and the "levering up" movement will become clearer.

Give it time. Success will come. I managed to teach my mare Monodie to Sit incredibly quickly because, prior to starting, I taught her to be instantaneously obedient to the "Whoa, halt," command in every gait. As she began to lever herself up from the outstretched-forelegs position, I spontaneously called out "Whoa, halt," and to my surprise, she stopped in the sitting position! Naturally, I praised her and so the trick was learned at the first attempt.

You, too, can train this as an intermediate step. Practice stopping from the walk and trot in-hand. Ask for a halt as your horse is moving backward or sideways. Mix it up. In other words, interrupt the current movement—whatever it may be—with a halt command. Then reinforce this obedience to "Whoa, halt," with work on the longe line, and deepen it with work under saddle. With this preliminary work, you will be able to stop your horse from jumping to his feet from the Lying Down or Sitting positions with a simple vocal command.

9 Ultimately, your horse will lever his front end up so high that it can be called Sitting. At this point you want to change the position of his forelegs so that they are centered in front of his hind legs. To do this, stand on the same side as the hind legs are pointing and offer your horse treats held progressively closer to you until he comes into the desired position.

If your horse does not understand what you want, work with a second person again. Stand at the horse's withers holding the reins wide apart. Use neck-rein and opening-rein signals to help guide your horse in the right direction while your assistant coaxes him with food. Once your horse has realized that he should place his forelegs so that they are centered between his hind legs, you again try adjusting his position on your own, with treats rather than rein pressure.

10 Work toward performing this trick at liberty. Ben knows this exercise very well. If I turn him loose in the arena, he rolls and then sits down, as though it were only fitting. Then he looks around to see if I am watching and stretches and twists his neck as though to say he has now surely earned a food reward.

The difference between your horse and Ben is that Ben already has many hours of practice behind him, hours that still lie ahead of you. But I am quite certain that with patience, kindness, and a sense of fun, one day you can train your horse well enough to show some professionals a thing or two.

Then, you will maybe find yourself sneaking out to the barn late at night, and unlocking your horse's stall door, leading him out to the arena with nothing but your hand upon his neck. There perhaps you will put on some music, practice your tricks one-by-one and even integrated into a little routine, and then, while the music is still playing to maintain the mood, you will sit down and savor the moment.

Wonderful!

› Something More I Want to Say

You may have noticed that Spanish Walk—which I mention often throughout the book—was not included in the step-by-step instructional section. It is surely a classic trick, but unfortunately there simply was not enough space to give careful, detailed descriptions of the steps to teaching your horse this movement.

Also for reasons of lack of space, I resisted relentlessly cheering you on and then rejoicing with you over each small success. I would gladly have done that but I had to struggle for each line. So in my parting words, I wish you these results: that your relationship with your horse becomes many times more enlightened; that you both gain in self-confidence and pride; and that you receive recognition from barnmates, friends, family, and others for what you have accomplished alongside your horse.

I created this book only because I want to give you ways to make the often boring and difficult work of training a riding horse a loving and joyful experience—for both human and horse. So, ideally, I would glean from you a promise that you will, in the future, take it upon yourself to make changes in the other work you do with your horse, using some of the techniques and theories you use for teaching tricks to make all work with your horse fun.

Allow me yet one more thought. Tricks may be mocked by some, and called "poodle dressage" or dismissed as a lower form of equestrian art. But the training philosophy of my husband, the dressage rider and trainer Philippe Karl, begins with the basic premise, "Art must respect nature." In every kind of work with animals—in our case with horse—the question arises whether we have the right to do it. My answer is "Yes," we have the right to pursue this "lower form of equestrian art" if the horse is trained with as much gentleness as possible and is cherished and respected as our most valued partner. That alone elevates the discipline pursued, whatever it may be, to a thing of beauty and worthy of the utmost respect.

The horse must never be enslaved, and our power, ownership, or other interests must never work to the horse's detriment.

Endeavor to make your horses "laugh with joy" in their work, and allow them the chance to shine.

Yours,

Bea Borelle

Index

> Index

Names of tricks are italicized.
Pages with photos are italicized.

Above/behind the bit, 23, *23*
Advanced tricks. *See* Brave horse tricks
Age of horse, optimal for training, 1–2
Arenas, 5
Atmosphere, importance of, 25, *26*
Atop the Mountain, 11, *15–16*, *15–17*
Audiences, achievement goal for, 12–13

Backing-Up, *50–52*, *50–53*
Balance Beam, *76–77*, *76–77*
Basic tricks, 47–54
Benefits of tricks
    achievement goals and, 12–13
    and basics for riders, 41, *41–45*, *44–45*
    gymnastic, 10–12
    self-confidence in horse, 4, 39
Bombproof horse tricks
    In Motion with "Racket Sack", *60–61*, *60–61*
    Riding without a Bridle, *56–57*, *56–57*
    Statue with Buckets, *64–66*, *64–66*
    Statue with "Racket Sack", *58–59*, *58–59*
    Statue with Sheet, 67–68, *67–68*
    Statue with Umbrella, *62–63*, *62–64*
Bow
    equipment for, 6
    as gymnastic training, 10
    Lying Down ("Upright" or "Awake") from the One-Legged Bow, 118–119
    One-Legged Bow to Lying Down ("Upright" or "Awake"), 119–125
    One-Legged Bow versus cleaning hooves, 111
    One-Legged Bow (with "Leg Rope"), 107–112, *108–109*, *111–112*
    One-Legged Bow (without "Leg Rope"), 103–106, *104–106*
    rewards for, 10
Brave horse tricks
    Balance Beam, *76–77*, *76–77*
    Ribbon Wall, *70–72*, *70–73*
    Standing on Pallets/Pedestal, *73–75*, *73–75*
    Tightrope, *78–79*, *78–79*
Breeds, optimal for training, 3
Buckets, *64–66*, *64–66*

Carpet, unrolling/rolling-up, 14, *82–86*, *83–86*
Carrying Objects, *89–91*, *89–92*
Circles, volte, 19–23, *20–23*
Classic horse tricks
    Kneeling, 113–115, *114*
    Leg rope, 120–123
    Lying Down ("Flat" or "Asleep"), 126–127, *126–127*
    Lying Down (remaining), 124–125, *124–125*
    Lying Down ("Upright" or "Awake"), 115, *115–118*
    Lying Down ("Upright" or "Awake") from the One-Legged Bow, 118–119
    Lying Down ("Upright" or "Awake") with the Leg Rope, 119–125, *120–123*
    One-Legged Bow to Lying Down ("Upright" or "Awake"), 119–125
    One-Legged Bow (with "Leg Rope"), 107–112, *108–109*, *111–112*
    One-Legged Bow (without "Leg Rope"), 103–106, *104–106*
    Plié, 97–102, *98–102*
    Sitting, 128–131, *128–131*
Commands, *31*
    importance of consistency, 30–31
    verbal/vocal, 32
Communication
    as benefit, 13
    importance of, 17

nonverbal/verbal, 31, *31*
Connections, establishment of, 38–39, *39*
Covers, *92–93*
Crossing the Forelegs, 81–82, 81–82

Dressage
    Spanish Walk and, 12, 132
Duration of training, 30, 42. *See also specific trick, i.e.*
    Carrying Objects

Equipment. *See also specific trick, i.e.*
    Carrying Objects
    food rewards, 7–10, *9*
    for the horse, 6
    for the trainer, 6–7, *8*
Errors/mistakes
    incorrect order of lying down, 123
    lying down without being asked, 112
    no head/neck bend when lying down, 119
    not controlling which side lying down
        occurs on, 118
    not lying down on cue, 117
    regression and, 39
    rolling instead of lying down, 123
    at volte, 19–23
Exercises. *See also* Trick training
    repetitions for, 42

Facilities
    atmosphere, 25
    footing conditions, 5
    training spaces, 5
Falls out/in with hindquarters, at volte, 21–23, 23
Feeding discipline as training tool, *27,* 27–28
Flexing, *23*
Food rewards?, 7–10
Food rewards, *9,* 17, 26, *26,* 26
    feeding discipline and, *27,* 27–28

Footing conditions, 5
On the forehand, 23, *23*

Gender, optimal for training, 3

Halting on command, 130
Health, optimal for training, 3–4
Heavy in the hands, *23,* 23
Hindquarters, falls out/in with, 23
Humorous horse tricks
    Carrying Objects, 89–91, 89–92
    Under the Covers, 92–93, 92–93
    Crossing the Forelegs, 81–82, 81–82
    Nudging and Pushing, 87–88, 87–88
    Unrolling and Rolling-Up Carpet, 14, 82–86,
        83–86
    Unsaddled, 94–95, *94–95*

Ignoring as training tool, 29
Intelligence
    development of, 12
    optimal for training, *3*
Intensity of training, 30

Karl, Philippe, 23, 132
Kneeling, 113–115, *114*

Lateral movements, *10,* 11
Lead ropes, 6, *7*
Leg rope, 6
    *Lying Down ("Upright" or "Awake") with the Leg
        Rope,* 119–125, *120–123*
    One-Legged Bow (with "Leg Rope"), 107–112,
        108–109, 111–112
Leg wraps, 6
Leisure Riders Test Center (Germany), 5
Longe lines, 6, *7*

Lying Down
    equipment for, 6
    remaining, *124–125, 124–125*
Lying Down ("Flat" or "Asleep"), 126–127, 126–127
Lying Down "Flat" to Lying Down "Upright", 127
Lying Down ("Upright" or "Awake")
    with the Leg Rope, 119–125, *120–123*
    from the One-Legged Bow, 118–119
    from the Roll, *115*, 115–118

Neck ring, *44*
Nudging and Pushing, 87–88, *87–88*

One-Legged Bow to Lying Down ("Upright" or
    "Awake"), 119–125
One-Legged Bow (with "Leg Rope"), 107–112,
    108–109, 111–112
    versus cleaning hooves, 111
One-Legged Bow (without "Leg Rope"), 103–106,
    104–106

Pallets, 73–75, *73–75*
Panic snaps, 6
Pausing as training tool, 28, *28*
Pedestal, 73–75, *73–75*
Piaffe-pirouette, *5*
Plié
    as classic trick basic, 97–102, *98–102*
    equipment for, 6
    rewards for, 10
    spontaneous, 102
Pointing pirouette, 35
Ponies as optimal for training, *2*
Positive reinforcement, 17. *See also* Rewards
    and trick training ramifications for riding, 18
Praise. *See also* Rewards
    food rewards, 7–10, *9, 17, 26,* 26
    "hands-on", *25*, 25

riding ramifications and, 18–19
    verbal, *25,* 25
Punishment, 29, 94. *See also* Errors/mistakes

Racket Sack
    motion with, 60–61, *60–61*
    Statue with, *58–59, 58–59*
Rearing, 3, 31
Relationship with horse, 12
Repetitions. *See* Duration of training
Rewards
    and basics for riders, 41
    feeding discipline and, *27*, 27–28
    food, 7–10, *9, 17, 26, 26*
    Lying Down (remaining) and, 124
    praise, 18–19
    pyramid of, 44
Ribbon Wall, 13, 70–72, 70–73
    bridleless through, 45
Riding
    Lying Down and, 120
    One-Legged Bow (with "Leg Rope") and, 110
    One-Legged Bow (without "Leg Rope") and, 103
    Plié and, 98
    trick training ramifications for, 18–23
Riding without a Bridle, 45
    for bombproof horses, *56–57,* 56–57
    through *Ribbon Wall,* 45
Round pens, 5

Sacking out, 72
Safety, as achievement goal, 13
Sheets, *67–68,* 67–68
Shipping boots, 6
Shoulders, falls out/in with, 23
Side-Stepping toward You, 53–54, *53–54*
Signals. *See also* Commands
    determining, 13

and phases of training (overview), *14*
  specificity of, 16–17
Sitting, 128–131, 128–131
  equipment for, 6
Size of horse, optimal for training, 3
Soundness. *See also* Health
  optimal for training, 3–4
  tricks for unsound/rehabilitating horse, 4
Spanish Walk
  importance of, 132
  and improvement of dressage, 12
  and "on"/"off" switches, 33, *36*
  Tellington Method lead ropes and, 6
Speed, at volte, 19–21
Standing on Pallets/Pedestal, 73–75, 73–75
Starting point to end goal, 37–38, *38*
Statue, 6, 47–49, 47–49
Statue with Buckets, 64–66, 64–66
Statue with Sheet, 67–68, 67–68
Statue with Umbrella, 62–63, 62–64

Tack. *See* Equipment
Temperament/intelligence, optimal for training, *3*
Tightrope, 78–79, 78–79
Trainer
  qualities of, *35*
  recognition of work of, 12–13
Training spaces, 5
Training tools
  differentiating between exercises, 33
  establishment of connections, 38–39, *39*
  feeding discipline and, *27*, 27–28
  ignoring, 29
  and "on"/"off" switches, 33–36, *36*
  pausing, *28*, 28
  punishment, 29
  sacking out, 72
  saying "No", 33

Trick training. *See also* Bombproof horse tricks;
    Brave horse tricks; Classic horse tricks;
      Humorous horse tricks
  Backing-Up, 50–52, 50–53
  Balance Beam, 76–77, 76–77
  basic exercises for, 47–54
  basic training as prerequisite, 4–5
  benefits of, *4*, 10–12
  Carrying Objects, 89–91, 89–92
  choice of trick, 36
  Under the Covers, 92–93, 92–93
  Crossing the Forelegs, 81–82, 81–82
  defined, 1
  duration/intensity of, 30
  images of starting/end points for, 37–38, *38*
  importance of, 132
  Kneeling, 113–115, 114
  Lying Down ("Flat" or "Asleep"), 126–127, 126–127
  Lying Down (remaining), 124–125, 124–125
  Lying Down ("Upright" or "Awake"), 115, 115–118
  *Lying Down ("Upright" or "Awake") from the
      One-Legged Bow, 118–119*
  *Lying Down ("Upright" or "Awake") with the
      Leg Rope, 119–125, 120–123*
  In Motion with "Racket Sack", 60–61, 60–61
  Nudging and Pushing, 87–88, 87–88
  *One-Legged Bow to Lying Down ("Upright"
      or "Awake"), 119–125*
  *One-Legged Bow (with "Leg Rope"), 107–112,
      108–109, 111–112*
  *One-Legged Bow (without "Leg Rope"), 103–106,
      104–106*
  phases of (overview), *14*
  Plié, 97–102, 98–102
  ramifications for riding, 18–23
  reasons for, 12–13
  Ribbon Wall, 70–72, 70–73
  Riding without a Bridle, 56–57, 56–57

   Side-Stepping toward You, 53–54, *53–54*
   Sitting, *128–131*, 128–131
   Standing on Pallets/Pedestal, 73–75, *73–75*
   Statue, 47–49, *47–49*
   Statue with Buckets, 64–66, 64–66
   Statue with "Racket Sack", 58–59, *58–59*
   Statue with Sheet, 67–68, 67–68
   Statue with Umbrella, 62–63, 62–64
   Tightrope, 78–79, *78–79*
   Unrolling and Rolling-Up Carpet, 82–86, *83–86*
   Unsaddled, 94–95, *94–95*
Tellington Method lead ropes, 6

Umbrellas, *62–63*, *62–64*
Unrolling and Rolling-Up Carpet, 14, *82–86*,
   83–86
Unsaddled, 94–95, *94–95*

Verbal commands. *See* Commands
Volte, 19–23, *20–23*

Whips/crops, 6, *7*